Asprey & Garrard

LONDON

TRAVELS WITH THE PRINCE

A Fiftieth Birthday Exhibition

selected by

His Royal Highness The Prince of Wales

In aid of The Prince of Wales's Charitable Foundation

This publication has been produced to
accompany the exhibition *Travels with the Prince*
shown at Hampton Court Palace
14 November 1998 – 28 February 1999
in aid of The Prince of Wales's Charitable Foundation.

Published 1998 by Sheeran Lock
ISBN 1 900123 20 7

A catalogue record for this publication is available
from the British Library

Catalogue edited by Imogen Lock
Editorial Assistant Sara Hill
Photography of artworks by Richard Littlewood
Designed by Lloyd Fishwick Associates
Printed by The Wolsey Press, Suffolk

Exhibition selected by HRH The Prince of Wales
Organised by Sheeran Lock
Curated by John Sheeran
Designed by Charles Marsden-Smedley

Advisory Group:
Christian Bailey, Office of HRH The Prince of Wales
Robin Evans, Historic Royal Palaces
Michael Fawcett, Office of HRH The Prince of Wales
Imogen Lock, Sheeran Lock
Maria Sealy, Asprey & Garrard
Manon Williams, Office of HRH The Prince of Wales

Cover illustration:
HRH The Prince of Wales
Greek Landscape, Summer (ii) 1996 watercolour (detail, Cat. 33)

Contents

Contents

Foreword

by His Royal Highness The Prince of Wales

When it was suggested that I might like to select an art exhibition to celebrate my 50th birthday, I was delighted to have an opportunity to share some of the pleasure that art and the friendship of artists has given me over the years. The result, ***Travels with the Prince*** includes some of my own watercolours, works by artists with whom I have travelled and fifty winning and selected entries for my Young Artists' Award. This latter is a splendidly imaginative initiative which has produced some interesting and rewarding interpretations of Britain today, which feature in a companion catalogue.

Whenever I can I try to snatch an opportunity to record my impressions of landscapes in different parts of the world. Since 1985, I have also persuaded some outstanding British artists to accompany me on official tours overseas and they have risked life and limb, and every kind of hazard, to do the same. The results have, I hope, been beneficial for both of us. I must say that having artists around makes life much more interesting and amusing and I can only trust that it has been worthwhile for those artists who have been with me, and perhaps helped them in their careers. Inevitably one can only choose a fraction of the total output, but in this exhibition I have chosen some of my favourite works, most of which I have acquired for my own collection.

It gives me particular pleasure that ***Travels with the Prince*** is being held in the Cartoon Gallery at Hampton Court Palace. Not only was this one of the first purpose-built picture galleries in Britain, being designed by Sir Christopher Wren, but the Palace itself also contains a wealth of pictures from the Royal Collection, and has a very special atmosphere of its own. Moreover, I am delighted that the proceeds from the exhibition are going to my own Charitable Foundation, which distributes money to charities with which I am particularly concerned: those working with young people, in the field of healthcare, the arts, heritage and environment.

Many people and organisations have helped to make this exhibition a success. In particular, I should like to thank Asprey & Garrard, for supporting the project and giving so much advice; Historic Royal Palaces for providing such a splendid venue and Sheeran Lock for organising the exhibition. Last, but not least, I would like to thank all the contributing artists who have added so much to my understanding and appreciation of art, and have made my official tours abroad with them such a delight.

Charles

Preface

by Ian Dahl, Chairman and Chief Executive, Asprey & Garrard

We at Asprey & Garrard are honoured to support ***Travels with the Prince*** and the ***Young Artists' Britain*** art award in celebration of the fiftieth birthday of HRH The Prince of Wales.

Leaders in the luxury goods market for over 200 years, Asprey and Garrard, two great English names, were united in September 1998. Each has enjoyed the highest acclaim for its jewellery, silver-work, special commissions and objets d'art: and it is these standards of craftsmanship and technical excellence that Asprey & Garrard will take forward to the next millennium.

It is the sheer diversity of skills that makes ***Travels with the Prince*** and the ***Young Artists' Britain*** art award such a joy to support, and such a worthwhile acknowledgement of the artistic talent of HRH The Prince of Wales, his tour artists, and the young people of Great Britain today.

Travels with the Prince

by Susan Morris

Royal Patronage

Public duty and private enthusiasm: royal patronage of the arts has always had a personal element. The French Ambassador Jean du Bellay, writing to Francis I in 1532, caught the note of delight in Henry VIII's voice as he took him round each palace building project: 'He shows it to me and tells me what he has done, and what he is going to do'.[1] And there is no doubting the joy that Queen Victoria derived from art. Her watercolour teacher William Leighton Leitch described the recently widowed Queen painting at Balmoral in 1863: 'I wish you could have seen us . . . Her Majesty sitting in the middle of a country road, with a great rough stone out of the river to put her paint box on . . . There was lots of talking, and laughing, and nearly two hours passed away very soon – the Queen remarking how quickly the time flew when she was drawing'.[2]

The exhibition ***Travels with the Prince*** reflects the public and the private side of HRH The Prince of Wales's interest in art. Over 50 paintings have been selected from the work of 10 artists who have travelled with the Prince on official royal tours. They are shown with 50 of the Prince's own watercolours, many from private painting expeditions. The third section of the exhibition shows another aspect of the Prince's patronage: his encouragement of art education. It brings together 50 winning and highly commended works submitted to *HRH The Prince of Wales's Young Artists' Award*, established to encourage young people to draw and paint and to record their impressions of Britain today.

The setting for the exhibition, the Cartoon Gallery at Hampton Court Palace, is a reminder of the prodigious enthusiasm of a long line of royal collectors. It was built for William III in 1699 by Sir Christopher Wren and William Talman, to house the precious Raphael Cartoons, acquired by Charles I with the Duke of Mantua's collection in 1626. Rubens (who painted the ceiling of the Banqueting House in Whitehall), called Charles I 'The greatest amateur of paintings among the princes of the world'.[3]

Charles I began collecting Italian paintings when still Prince of Wales, encouraged by the legacy of his elder brother Henry, Prince of Wales. Prince Henry had built up an exquisite collection of Italian painting and sculpture before his death in 1612, aged 18. Charles I's collection, including works by Raphael, Titian and Mantegna, rivalled the finest in Europe before it was broken up by the Commonwealth after his execution.

Another Prince of Wales who made his artistic mark was Frederick, Prince of Wales, son of George II and father of George III. He encouraged the flourishing of the Rococo in England, patronising painters such as Jacopo Amigoni and Philip Mercier as well as silversmiths such as Paul de Lamerie and Nicholas Sprimont. The informal, lighthearted tenor of this taste is epitomised by Mercier's conversation piece of Frederick Prince of Wales and his sisters playing music in the gardens at Kew, 1733.

George III's love of art – he was a talented draughtsman – encompassed an eye for landscape painting which matched his love of the English landscape and interest in agricultural improvements (three interests shared with Prince Albert and the present Prince of Wales). George III created a 'landscape room' at Buckingham House, acquired some of Canaletto's finest works and spurred the watercolour painter Paul Sandby to create a poetic series of Windsor views.

The future George IV, while Prince of Wales, rebelled against his father's taste for simplicity by creating some of the most opulent

Fig. 1 HRH The Prince of Wales painting in Bhutan 1998

interiors commissioned by any Prince at Carlton House and the Royal Pavilion, Brighton. He was the catalyst for an outpouring of creativity, his age epitomised by Lawrence's glamorous portraits just as Van Dyck had captured the court of Charles I.

Queen Victoria and Prince Albert encouraged many public art and design projects, notably the 1851 Great Exhibition and plans for the South Kensington museums. Art was also a much valued private pursuit: between them, they practised drawing, painting, etching, sculpture and architecture (Prince Albert designed the new royal residence of Osborne on the Isle of Wight). The Queen's enthusiasm for painting was unprecedented, as was her patronage of landscape watercolourists. She took lessons from Edward Lear and William Leighton Leitch, fascinated by their experience of Italy and their panoramic, high-coloured, fervent response to landscape. Edwin Landseer, too, gave the Queen lessons and was invited to paint with the royal party at Balmoral, the Highland haven where Queen Victoria had first spent the summer in 1848. Her rapturous response to the Highland landscape, both in words and in pictures, finds echoes in the present Prince of Wales's own watercolours.

Fig. 2 Queen Victoria *Ardverickie Lodge* 1847 (The Royal Collection)

Formative influences on the Prince of Wales's love of painting can be found in his immediate family. The Duke of Edinburgh is a keen painter. A huge influence on the Prince of Wales has been his grandmother Queen Elizabeth The Queen Mother, who nurtured his early artistic interests. Her own collection includes exquisite Impressionist paintings by Monet, Morisot and Fantin-Latour, among others; she also owns a fine collection of 20th century British paintings which cherishes the British Romantic landscape tradition. Some of these works were acquired through her friendship with artists such as Edward Seago and John Piper.

The Queen Mother's collection could not bear better witness to a belief in the eternal, civilising value of art despite the vicissitudes of history. A group of watercolours of Windsor Castle by Piper and Paul Nash's *Landscape of the Vernal Equinox* were acquired by King George VI and Queen Elizabeth in the darkest days of the Second World War. Piper's view of the Round Tower, Windsor, overhung with storm clouds, reflects the English Romantic watercolour at its most dark and yet most defiant (Fig. 3). Windsor becomes both a beloved home and a national symbol. Compare these Piper drawings with Thomas Sandby's sunny Windsor views for George III or the Prince of Wales's commissioned paintings of the developing gardens at Highgrove – royal life, public and private, is woven into royal art collecting.

Patron and Collector

HRH The Prince of Wales has explained why he began painting landscape watercolours: 'I wanted to create something with more texture and life than you can with photographs. I used to take a camera with me on tours, but I found photos rather flat; they don't give a sense of feeling the landscape. I had the urge to express what I saw in paint'.

A keen painter since his teens, the Prince has built up a fine collection of British art and artists have become mentors, friends and travelling companions. This exhibition brings together over 50 works by 10 artists who have travelled with the Prince; their work brings a unique insight to the experience of a royal tour which a camera could not capture.

The idea of asking artists to accompany him on tours abroad was prompted by the Prince's desire to 'keep the Royal Collection alive'.[4] He recollects: 'When I was a child at Windsor I started noticing the pictures along the grand corridors; they were mostly of friends, wives, dogs, horses, houses of previous monarchs or Princes of Wales. It seemed to me that the interest lay in the idiosyncrasies, the way of life of those people. The artists I commission are making a record of contemporary life, travelling with me. It's not a representative museum collection, it's something that reflects the age and individual taste'.

The Prince's systematic policy of taking an artist on tour seems to be unique among British royalty, though Queen Victoria invited artists including Landseer to sketch with her in Scotland. Whether formally, through teaching him, or less consciously, through working side by side with him, artists have influenced the Prince's life as a painter.

The Prince's private art collection is diverse, but reflects in a satisfying way his interests and philosophies. Most of his commissioned artists have had a formal training at one of the old-established art schools, such as the Royal Academy or the Slade. Good drawing and sound painting technique underpin their creativity – discipline which the Prince applauds, and which he often discusses with artists on tour.

Given his love of country life and environmental concerns, it is unsurprising that landscape painting is richly represented in the Prince's collection. Artists like Derek Hill and Peter Greenham (Fig. 8) are part of a British Romantic tradition in which painterliness, economy of form and emotional engagement with the landscape are paramount. Both took part in the National Trust Foundation for Art *Salute to Turner* exhibition (1989), in which the Prince took a keen interest. (Like the Prince, the Foundation sustains the patronage of British art by commissioning new works for the Trust's country houses).

City views by John Sergeant and John Ward reflect the Prince's oft-stated belief that the best architecture expresses and uplifts the human spirit. And in a long tradition of royal portrait commissions, Peter Kuhfeld's portraits of Princes William and Harry stand apart for their sensitivity and informality. Other portraits in the Prince's collection – by Emma Sergeant, Susannah Fiennes and Martin Yeoman, among others – express the diversity, dignity and grace of the anonymous individuals encountered on his worldwide tours.

There is also the Prince's delight in the quirky, lyrical aspect of British painting – in John Napper's Arcadian visions of Shropshire,

Fig. 3 John Piper
The West End of the Upper Ward with the Round Tower, Windsor Castle 1942
(Collection of HM Queen Elizabeth The Queen Mother)

or the magic that Napper conjures from objects in works such as his large watercolour *Still Life with Mandolin and Pheasant Feather* 1988 (Fig. 5).

One of the earliest influences on the Prince's painting was the Norfolk artist Edward Seago, a friend of King George VI and Queen Elizabeth whose work is well represented in the Queen Mother's collection. Seago's windswept panoramas of East Anglia, as well as his steel-blue, cool green and silvery palette, find echoes in watercolours by the Prince such as *Landscape, Sandringham* 1995 (Cat. 47). The Prince usually paints at Sandringham in January; Seago excelled in painting brink-of-spring days with leaden clouds and sodden furrows.

Like the work of Constable, his great East Anglian predecessor, Seago's oils are both Romantic and naturalistically observed: the free impasto of his cloudscapes is underpinned by a study of meteorology. He was an astonishingly assured watercolourist: 'I stood behind him, lost in wonder, as a stunning watercolour emerged as if by magic – and entirely from his memory', the Prince has ruefully written.[5]

Another long-standing inspiration is the distinguished portrait painter Derek Hill, whom the Prince of Wales first met when Hill painted him as an undergraduate at Trinity College, Cambridge. The Prince owns several oil on board landscapes by Hill, the small size of which belie their sweeping, monumental simplicity. *Tory Island: West to the Lighthouse* 1975 (Cat. 64), a band of coastline caught between glittering sea and luminous sky, depicts an island off the coast of Donegal, where Derek Hill has lived for 40 years. Quite different in handling from Hill's shrewdly observed portraits, these oil sketches (like Landseer's small Highland oil sketches) seem to represent an unfettering of the imagination, distilling the essence of much-loved but ever-changing terrain. They exult in landscape which is (almost) unpeopled, unspoilt and untamable.

In 1995, the Prince painted the Mayo landscape in the company of Derek Hill. 'He has a wonderful eye', comments the Prince. Hill has long been one of the Prince's closest artistic mentors, both as a practical painting companion full of forthright advice, and as a wise recommender of artists for royal tours.

The Prince often invites old painting friends to Sandringham and Balmoral. 'Artists are the easiest of guests – they just want to go off and get on with their painting', the Prince remarks. The landscape of Balmoral cast a special spell on the Norwich-born 'School of London' painter Michael Andrews. He accompanied the Prince deer-stalking and made a superb sketch of the Prince's favourite waterfall not long before his death in 1995.

The Prince's interest in architecture is both passionate and catholic, a fact reflected in his collections and in his own work. Whether looking at European or non-European architecture, he responds to a respect for tradition, to sympathetic materials, to a human sense of scale.

The Prince's interest in Islamic architecture has been fired by

Fig. 4 Derek Hill
Queen Elizabeth The Queen Mother and The Prince of Wales Leaving Sandringham for the Fête 1995
(Collection of HM Queen Elizabeth The Queen Mother)

private painting trips to Turkey and Morocco with Derek Hill, as well as by official Middle Eastern tours. In 1986, Martin Yeoman accompanied the Prince to the Gulf. Invited back to the region, Yeoman managed to paint in Yemen, much to the envy of the Prince. 'I have a passion for Yemeni mud-brick architecture', the Prince admits. 'The buildings seem to grow out of the ground, and their decorative tradition is unique'.

Much nearer to home, a treasured possession is Sir Hugh Casson's watercolour sketch *Highgrove under Snow* c.1984 (Fig. 7). A skin of even wash plays winter sunlight across Highgrove's pale gold Cotswold stone. Sir Hugh's painting conveys the harmony and proportion of the Georgian building, seen from a corner of the garden which metamorphoses in summer into a meadow of wildflowers.

Sir Hugh, who gave the Prince of Wales painting and drawing lessons, would sketch, remarks the Prince, 'in the same way that other people hum tunes'.[6] One valuable Casson tip was that a weak composition can be saved by cropping – done to powerful effect in the Prince's close-up of *Cypress Trees in Provence* 1995 (Cat. 3).

The Prince has also gained advice from another superb draughtsman, John Ward. Ward was the very first official artist to travel with the Prince, visiting Italy with him on a royal tour in April and May 1985. The Prince's collection includes Ward's sketches from *HMY Britannia* (a subject which has caught the eye of many artists who have travelled with him). Studies of Venice from the Royal Yacht (Cat. 53, 55) attest to John Ward's understanding of Italian architecture, a frequent point of discussion with the Prince.

One of John Ward's letters to the Prince is illustrated with a delicate sketch of a street scene in Orvieto (Cat. 56), and the exclamation 'Goodness how amazing Italy is – what engineers!' For the Prince, who did not visit Italy until he was 36, primed by his grandmother's rapturous descriptions of travelling there in her youth, Italy was a revelation, a country where 'art....seems to invade every aspect of life'.[7] He returns there privately to paint and explore the art and architecture.

The ongoing dialogue between the Prince and his artists is reflected in numerous letters enlivened with illustrations. John Ward's son Toby, who accompanied the Prince to the Gulf States in 1993, sent a six-page illustrated letter crowded with his impressions (Cat. 88). Ward comments on the overwhelming beauty of Petra, (immortalised in David Roberts's 19th century lithographs, which line a hallway at Highgrove), and the awesome flatness of the Kuwaiti desert. He writes of the myriad colours of Arabia's Empty Quarter, first crossed by a Westerner (Ward's hero Wilfred Thesiger) in the 1940s.

The interior and still life painter John Sergeant sends letters (Cat. 78) which are outpourings of quirky, intense observation – not unlike his drawings in the Prince's collection, which have a Samuel Palmeresque honesty and delight in recording the world. (He was invited to paint at Sandringham and accompanied the Prince to the former Czechoslovakia in 1991.)

Fig. 5 John Napper
Still Life with Mandolin and Pheasant Feather 1988
(Collection of HRH The Prince of Wales)

Sergeant's watercolour *Teapot with Lustre Cup* (Fig. 6) raises the contemplation of everyday objects to a plane of spiritual serenity. Another drawing dissects the appearance of a pair of Edwardian scales; a third frames the landscape through a window at Sandringham.

Portraits have always been an important aspect of royal patronage, but the Prince deplores the lifelessness of much modern portraiture. Peter Kuhfeld was recommended to him by Sir Brinsley Ford, the connoisseur, collector and National Trust advisor who has been the catalyst for several of the Prince's commissions. Kuhfeld has painted the Prince in his Garter robes and two delightful, informal portraits of Princes William and Harry. In 1990 he accompanied the Prince on official visits to Nigeria and Cameroon; the haunting portrait *Young Girl in a Blue Dress, Umuagbai Village, Nigeria* (Cat. 73) is one fruit of this trip. Another is one of the most ambitious oils to derive from the Prince's tours, a durbar in Nigeria (Cat. 71). Kuhfeld orchestrates a huge crowd of dazzling figures under the African sun, catching the exuberance of people in the procession passing before the Prince.

Below left: Fig. 6 John Sergeant
Teapot with Lustre Cup 1992
(Collection of HRH The Prince of Wales)

Below right: Fig. 7 Sir Hugh Casson
Highgrove under Snow c.1984
(Collection of HRH The Prince of Wales)

Fig. 8 Peter Greenham
San Giovanni e Paulo from the Palatine c.1958-61
(Collection of HRH The Prince of Wales)

The estate at Highgrove, where the Prince of Wales farms 1,112 acres organically and where he has created an enchanting garden, has been well served by his patronage of artists. In 1988 Diana Armfield was invited to Highgrove and was delighted to find herself talking to the Prince about conservation and environmental issues dear to both of them. The Prince owns a number of oils by Armfield of Highgrove in spring. Her painterly brushwork and delicate, clear colours conjure up gardens just bursting into bloom: the velvety, pale green leaves of apple trees set against a white gate; the purple-grey branches and purple buds of wisteria framing the drawing room window.

Armfield's work catches the spirit of the gardens at Highgrove, created over the past decade with the advice of plantswomen such as Rosemary Verey. Their design, in Diana Armfield's words, has a 'hint of both France and Italy in a traditional though quite special English . . . garden'.[8] Painting with flowers outside, hanging landscape paintings inside: the Prince of Wales has shaped Highgrove with an artist's eye.

Watercolours by HRH The Prince of Wales

The selection of watercolours in the exhibition represents 50 of the Prince of Wales's most recent works, from many aspects of his life. They are painted in varying conditions – some in holiday hours, when the most pressing question is how to catch the fleeting effects of a sunset or dodge a rainstorm. Others were made at the end of days packed with official duties, when there is a race to catch the fading of the light, and sometimes finished from memory. The Prince prefers, however, to paint *en plein air*, believing that one can express the essence of a landscape only by painting in it. 'While you're painting you have to feel the landscape as an emotional experience', he says. In this, he follows the founders of the Romantic watercolour tradition: Girtin dashing in the effect of Exeter Cathedral in a shower; Turner lashing himself to the mast of a ship to feel, as well as paint, a storm.

The Prince's watercolours cover an extraordinary breadth of terrain, from the mists of a Norfolk January to a broiling wadi in Oman, via the pristine peaks of the Alps. The Prince paints in pure watercolour, with little or no pencil underdrawing and little use of bodycolour (opaque pigment), again following the tradition of watercolour practised by Turner, Girtin and De Wint. Laying translucent, even watercolour washes – with little chance for cover-up if things go wrong – is terrifyingly difficult, while looking uncannily simple. Ideally, it is a skill which needs to be practised every day (something not possible in a busy royal schedule).

The Prince's treasured sailcloth and leather painting bag (a present from his staff, made by a sailmaker in *HMY Britannia*) is doggedly taken on every royal tour. At Balmoral, he goes for long walks in search of the right subject and light; abroad, painting spots are sometimes picked by car, in the vain hope of avoiding the press. The neatly organised contents of the bag include two wooden colour-boxes, brushes and waterpots. 'I restrict my palette somewhat', the Prince says. 'But I often experiment with new paints given to me by artists'.

The Prince's watercolour of *Tetbury Church from Highgrove* 1996 (Cat. 48) demonstrates the simple directness of his vision. The spire in sunlight and shadow is defined by two contrasting washes, the framing foreground trees by wet glazes of colour boldly intermingled.

The Prince usually paints at Sandringham, Norfolk, in January and April. The gently undulating terrain of East Anglia, its huge skies boiling with clouds, has inspired painters from Gainsborough and Constable to Munnings and Seago. The last is one of the Prince's favourite 20th century painters: he owns Seago's *Marsh Track Near Hickling* c.1962 (Fig. 9).

The palette of the Prince's *Landscape, Sandringham* 1995 (Cat. 47), with grey-blue undershadowed clouds, pale green winter wheat in the fields, and the warm, complex browns in the distant woods, owes a debt to Seago. The open-ended composition vividly evokes the vast, airy breadth of the countryside around Sandringham, with winter breezes blowing off the sea.

Norfolk Landscape in January 1997 (Cat. 49) is a study mostly in tones of brown and gold of the sunset countryside. The Prince prefers to paint 'either early morning or at sunset, when the light is most complex'. In his Norfolk view, mists rise along the parallel lines of hedgerows and copses, turning each into a ghostly stage-set backdrop. Working in pure watercolour, the Prince glazes one translucent colour over another: light shining between distant tree trunks, for example, is suggested by laying a darker brown over a beige wash. Fingers of shadow on the foreground fields are created by dragging the lightest of grey and brown washes across cream paper.

The hedgerows and copses, the result of hundreds of years of husbandry and game conservation, give character to this landscape and provide the structural patterns of the watercolour. It is easy to see that it was painted by someone who has walked the landscape and understands its management.

Mountains are a consistent theme in the Prince's work, notably the familiar ones around the Balmoral estate, which the Prince has described as 'truly ... God's country'.[9] Constantly changing, moulded by passing clouds, the mountains in his watercolours can take the guise of solid barriers or gauzy apparitions. Queen Victoria responded powerfully to the landscape around Balmoral and did some of her finest watercolours there, such as *Ardverickie Lodge* 1847

Fig. 9 Edward Seago
Marsh Track Near Hickling c.1962
(Collection of
HRH The Prince of Wales)

(Fig. 2). The countryside, as well as the Queen's enthusiasm, also drew forth works of Romantic power from Landseer, William Leighton Leitch and Carl Haag, artists she invited to sketch with her.

The familiarity and freedom of Balmoral have also inspired some of the Prince's best watercolours. One of the few places in the world where he can escape the click of camera shutters, the landscape is a balm to the soul. 'I've looked at it so long that it's embedded in my subconscious', he comments.

The Prince employs particular freedom and attack in his view *From Auchtavan towards Invercauld* 1995 (Cat. 10). The middle ground is defined by a forest of pines (so sculptural from a distance, so sinister and oppressive close to). The ravine tumbles toward the viewer in a cascade of multicoloured brushstrokes: rust, ochre, slate-grey, lilac, pink. The distant peaks seem as ethereal as the lowering clouds.

The Prince also paints the Alps, where he goes to ski each year. The inspiration for his mountain landscapes lies less with Turner's smouldering veils of Alpine colour than with earlier artists like John Robert Cozens and Francis Towne, who grappled with the problems of representing white on white in the watercolour medium.

Cozens crossed the Alps to Italy with William Beckford in 1782, when Alpine travel was still fraught with danger. He employed a grey-blue palette and left the white paper bare to create highlights, defining his terrain through lines and masses of trees.

The following century, the Alps were colonised for pleasure: Queen Victoria went to Switzerland for the first time on a private visit in 1868, and, enraptured, painted the mountains 'glowing in the setting sun, what is called here "Alpengluhen" '.[10]

The Prince's watercolour of *The Hüreli, Klosters, Switzerland (ii)* 1994 (Cat. 43), is an effective example of the 'less is more' tenet of watercolour painting practised by Cozens: the whole of the snowy foreground slope is defined by leaving the white watercolour paper untouched. Scattered pines and grey washes of shadow – warmer greys on the upper slopes where the sun still reaches – define the contours of the mountainside. The milky blueness of the sky (one even, unstreaked wash) is reflected back by the snow.

From the glacial hues of Klosters to the saturated colours of the Mediterranean: the Prince has painted extensively in France, Italy, Greece and Asia Minor. 'I love painting in France and Italy', he says. With a few judiciously chosen colours, he evokes the sharp shadows, dazzling sun-warmed stone and ochre hills of the South.

Like Cozens and Lear before him, the Prince has discovered the tantalising quality of an ancient coastline seen across a stretch of blue water. His *Monemvasia, Greece* 1994 (Cat. 23), is quite unusual in his work in its experimentation with an upright format. A fine line – reminiscent of the pen line which bounds Edward Lear's watercolour washes – evokes the crystalline clarity of the white villa in the sun. Perched below a sheer cliff, defended by the sea, the building seems both lonely and idyllic.

Mediterranean architecture intrigues the Prince in his Greek and Provençale watercolours: the *Monastery of St John the Divine, Patmos,* 1993 (Cat. 22) crowning its hilltop; the silhouette of the *Château Le Barroux, Provence (ii)* 1996 (Cat. 7) echoing the contours of the land. These ancient buildings have grown gracefully into their settings, with none of the abrupt transitions of much modern architecture. The Prince has written: 'how vitally important it is that man-made structures...are fitted into the overall picture with sensitivity and vision. It seems to me we can't go far wrong if we try to aspire to the principle that whatever development takes place should owe something to the well-trained artist's eye'.[11]

The timelessness of these Mediterranean landscapes – trees that suit the climate, sustainable farming methods – is celebrated in the green-and-gold *Provençale Landscape* 1994 (Cat. 2). There is a sense that the sun has rolled around these same cypresses, olive groves and vine terraces for a thousand years. In one of the most powerful watercolours of his Provençale series, the Prince fills the foreground with dark green cypresses, allowing a peep of sunlit hillside beyond (Cat. 3). He declares: 'I love painting cypresses – they have a lovely darkness, a wonderful shadow. They draw you into the landscape'.

The famous Victorian traveller-painters, such as David Roberts and Edward Lear, explored Asia Minor and the Middle East, evoking the relentless heat in hot ochre and purple watercolour washes, stumbling across massive temples on the outskirts of flyblown villages, Ozymandian relics of lost civilisations.

Air travel has taken away much of the arduousness and the awe of those journeys, but parts of the globe still retain their mystery. The Prince has been lucky enough to encounter some of these places – such as Oman and Bhutan – as part of official visits. He has painted several times in the Arabian desert, alongside Martin Yeoman in 1986, Toby Ward in 1993 and Susannah Fiennes in 1995. (Their varied responses form a fascinating record.) *Wadi Qaram from Sayq, Oman,* 1995 (Cat. 35) called forth one of the Prince's most intense, freely painted works. Blocks of colour and geometric crosshatchings express the soul of the rocky landscape.

In gentle contrast are the Prince's 1997 watercolours of Tanzania. These African landscapes are saturated with a light that is totally different in quality from his sunset landscapes of the Mediterranean. As so often in the Prince's paintings, careful observation of tree forms helps to characterise the scene. In the watercolour of *Ngorongoro from Hugo Hill, Serengeti Plains, Tanzania* 1997 (Cat. 37), a flat, shady tree is placed to echo the graceful line of the purple range of mountains rising beyond the

Fig. 10 David Roberts
Entrance to Petra 1839
(Collection of
HRH The Prince of Wales)

plain. In *Rufiji River from Mbuyuni Camp, Selous Game Reserve, Tanzania (i)* 1997 (Cat. 39), a single palm reflected in the river ties the composition together, and the reflected sunset flushes the whole page with pink. The sketch trails off at the left of the paper, giving the scene a dreamy, mirage-like effect.

Recently, the Prince has been experimenting with a slightly larger format and with using an initial colour-wash on his paper to unify the tone. Four watercolours of Balmoral, made in January 1998 (Cat. 15, 17, 18, 19), are subtle meditations on the same familiar terrain, each expressing a different mood and quality of light. Opalescent skies and colour-shadowed snow are painted with poetic fluency. 'The great secret of art is to humble the ego and to feel the landscape', says the Prince. 'It's almost a kind of sacred feeling for landscape'.

Tour Artists

His laminated badge reading 'Official Artist' is Robert Wraith's treasured souvenir of the 1997 royal tour of South Africa. For Wraith, like most of the painters, the call from a Private Secretary to ask if he might be free to accompany the Prince came out of the blue. 'I was in darkest Herefordshire', laughs Susannah Fiennes, when she was asked to think about packing for Oman.

Although some of his artistic friends are doyens such as John Ward and Derek Hill, many of the Prince's tour artists are younger painters still defining their direction. In private visits to exhibitions, and through projects such as being a selector of the *Discerning Eye* exhibition, the Prince follows the progress of emerging careers.

The Prince chooses his tour artists shrewdly, often asking one successful candidate to recommend a colleague. Technical prowess, speed of execution and general *sang froid* are a necessity. The Prince comments: 'There are not many artists who can do this type of work now, unlike the 19th century, when all those marvellous sketchers for *The Illustrated London News* recorded royal events with such vitality. Today, an artist like Robert Wraith can keep a scene alive'.

Left: Fig. 11 Susannah Fiennes and HRH The Prince of Wales painting in Oman 1995

Opposite: Fig. 12 Emma Sergeant *Ninib, Sumerian God* 1996 (Collection of HRH The Prince of Wales)

Emma Sergeant was asked to accompany the Prince to Egypt and Morocco in 1995. Her fascination with ancient civilisations, reflected in studies of Afghan peoples and monumental 'portraits' of Orpheus and other mythic archetypes (Fig. 12), made her a sensitive choice to sketch in Egypt.

Part of the excitement of being chosen as an Official Artist is that no-one knows quite how they are going to react – professionally and personally – to new landscapes and the hectic but militarily precise atmosphere of a royal tour. 'It was like a dream' is an often-heard comment. Emma Sergeant, daunted at first by the press flashbulbs, 'hid in museums' and made sketches of eerily calm Ancient Egyptian heads that hover between being archaeological records and living portraits. Toby Ward sketched in the hubbub of the Dubai Air Show: 'When I got down to it I was pleasantly surprised at what could be distilled from such chaotic scenes', he wrote to the Prince after the Gulf tour (Cat. 88).

Several of the Prince's artists have undertaken more than one tour, often widely contrasting. Susannah Fiennes travelled with

the Prince to Oman in 1995 and was invited to Hong Kong in 1997. She was no stranger to the stresses of travelling and painting. In 1994, after winning a BP Travel Award, Susannah spent two months in China. She painted portraits and the cities of the hinterland; the graceful, triangular shapes of slow-moving cyclists became one of her themes.

Even so, Susannah Fiennes was surprised by the pace and intensity of the four-day Oman visit, on the occasion of the 25th anniversary of the Sultan's rule: 'So much of it was spent in planes; you had to seize the opportunity to sketch whenever you could'. One striking pencil sketch shows the Prince working at 3am on the flight home, profiled in the sharp light of the reading lamp.

Susannah was charmed by the kindness of the Prince's staff and the freedom she was given to paint what and where she pleased: 'I'm used to working alone so it was great to feel part of a team'. The first day she visited the market in Muscat – a sea of male figures in shimmering lilac, chalk-blue and white robes – to sketch for two hours in intense heat. Her sketchbooks filled with quickly blocked-in watercolours of turbaned, craggy figures.

These have formed the basis for some of the most successful paintings of the whole trip, a series of separate, frieze-like watercolours of Omani men on tall, thin strips of paper, the figures reduced almost to abstract essentials (Cat. 95). They powerfully express the unique colours, the timeless human dignity, and the vibrant quality of Oman's light.

Painted in her London studio, these watercolours reflect Susannah's penchant for developing a theme away from the motif. She says the format of the royal tour was perfect for her way of working: 'I like to work in quick bursts of experience, gathering lots of images. Then the seed of an idea resonates from what I've done before'.

Susannah Fiennes also spent two evenings in the Omani landscape painting with the Prince. The desert was 'not at all what I had imagined – not rolling dunes and camels. It was gravel to infinity and a few shadows. So I painted the Prince painting. Alone, head bowed. It was very moving' (Cat. 96).

Her quasi-abstract watercolours of the Oman landscape are full of complex colour: gullies and rivulets of ochre, pink, terracotta washes shading one into the other. These runnels and rivulets are echoed in the faces of the Bedou whom Susannah encountered. The unforgiving terrain, where men have clung to survival for centuries, is suggested in the monumental oil heads of Omanis painted back in London. The same patient, dignified faces are captured in Martin Yeoman's portraits of Arabs (Cat. 58, 59).

Susannah Fiennes was impressed by how hard the Prince worked at his painting and how open he was to advice – for example, to strengthen the foreground in one of his desert watercolours. After the trip, she was invited to Highgrove to compare notes: 'He chose to keep some watercolours of men in Muscat market and some studies in different media of a man in a turban – good choices, I think'.

In June 1997 Susannah Fiennes was invited on one of the most significant trips the Prince has undertaken – the handover of Hong Kong to Chinese rule, which, poignantly, also marked the last official voyage of *HMY Britannia*. Fiennes's watercolours from the yacht (as do many works in the Prince's collection) give a sense of the magical, slightly dislocated view from this floating world. She recorded the bobbing flotilla of accompanying craft, the bulk of a warship motionless between the sea and sky of a grey dawn.

HMY Britannia herself features too, a triangle of rigging against the towering verticals of the Hong Kong harbour (Cat. 97). Reflected in the glass skyscrapers are steely clouds, which burst in a huge thunderstorm during the handover ceremony, so that Fiennes's sketches of the handover are imbued with the brightly coloured geometry of a thousand umbrellas.

A sketch of Christopher Patten, the last British Governor of Hong Kong, back turned, looking over the rail of *HMY Britannia* (Cat. 98), inspired the idea of an oil painting of the same composition. Fiennes says: 'It summed up the painful, overwhelming leavetaking of the colony, which everyone felt'.

Equally historic was the Prince of Wales's visit in 1997 to Southern Africa. It included meetings with President Mandela, whose State Visit to Britain was a particularly happy occasion.

The artist chosen for the nine-day tour was Robert Wraith, a Fellow of the Royal Society of Portrait Painters who is also known for his poised, painterly still lifes. Disciplined technique underpins the fluent, witty sketches that resulted from the South African tour, recording in pen, ink and wash days full of contrasts. Wraith, whether painting or drawing, works only in front of the motif, never from photographs: 'You live through the painting'.

One of his most touching works is a page of crayon studies made when the Prince was deep in conversation with President Mandela – two lively likenesses, just heads floating in the creamy white of the paper, that manage to convey more about an exchange of ideas than any photo could (Cat. 101). Wraith was seated diagonally across from the pair at a banquet, sketching discreetly. 'Did you manage to get a portrait of President Mandela?' the Prince asked anxiously when he next encountered his Official Artist.

Other sketches show the astonishing contrasts of the visit. While the Prince visited community projects in the shanty town of Crossroads near Cape Town – projects which echo the work of the Prince's Trust in Britain – Wraith sketched a young black man watching the royal party. Defined in a few wiry pen lines in front of a crumbling building, he is the observer observed (Cat. 105). 'I was sketching from the back of a van', says Wraith. 'People were crowding round, but I was invisible'.

Open another random page of the sketchbook, and one comes across the Prince at the Natural History Museum dwarfed by whale bones festooned from the ceiling. ('Hall of whales, how very appropriate', quipped the Prince.)

Open another page and there is the startlingly green valley at Isandhlwana, scene of the famous British defeat by the Zulus. While the royal party went on an historical tour of the area, Wraith perched on a rock and enjoyed a rare moment of solitary oil sketching. (The Prince, though taking his watercolour bag with him everywhere, found no time to paint on this trip.)

The royal party also travelled to the kingdom of Swaziland and attended the coronation of King Letsie III in nearby Lesotho. The ceremony – a grandstand view from the royal box – filled more pages of sketchbook (Cat. 100). Lines of gyrating dancers, in thumb-nail sketches barely an inch high, stamp their rhythm off the page. Here is old and new Africa together: tribesmen in skin cloaks and dazzling feather headdresses; King Letsie at the moment of coronation, resplendent in ceremonial robes, silhouetted before a grey barrage of microphones.

On his return Wraith had thirty of the best sketchbook leaves mounted and presented them to the Prince, who was delighted. When asked how the Prince's commission made a difference to him, Wraith says: 'The trip was a fantastic, dreamlike, overwhelming experience. And even if you are quite well established, it makes a difference to your career. People look at you in a different light'.

James Hart Dyke's compulsion to sketch served him well on a hectic royal tour to Sri Lanka, Nepal and Bhutan in February 1998. In England, he finds himself drawing on tube trains or even at parties. On tour, his lively pencil outlines captured every member of the Prince's team: Assistant Private Secretary Nick Archer was surreptitiously sketched during a briefing session ('He thought I was taking notes', James smiles.) The pencil and wash sketches unfold as a visual diary: a saffron umbrella waving above the crowds at Raja Maha Vihara temple, Sri Lanka; the Prince with the King of Nepal; a smiling Bhutani girl in graceful national dress.

The visit encompassed three very different Asian countries, beginning with Sri Lanka for celebrations marking the 50th anniversary of Independence. Security was exceptionally tight to counter the threat of Tamil Tiger guerrillas. To add to this pressure, the Prince's Official Artist was invited to a meeting with the President of Sri Lanka, where both he and the Prince showed their sketches, surrounded by a packed audience of dignitaries and press. Hart Dyke coped with admirable *sang froid*. He was impressed by his host's enthusiasm to see the Prince's watercolours and his own sketches of the tour: 'The works were clearly a symbol of the Prince's interest in the arts'.

The lush green tones of Sri Lanka were replaced by earth colours

Fig. 13 Robert Wraith sketching in South Africa 1997

Fig. 14 James Hart Dyke in Nepal 1998

and dazzling snow as the royal party journeyed on to Nepal and Bhutan. In Nepal, the Prince inspected conservation work at Kathmandu's Patan Durbar Square, a World Heritage site. Taking a day off from the official itinerary, Hart Dyke made oil sketches of Nepal's terraced valleys, and the breathtaking Himalayas blue-white in the morning sun (Cat. 107).

The Bhutan trip was the first-ever visit by a member of the British royal family to this Himalayan kingdom between India and China, ruled by English-educated King Jigme Singye Wangchuk. Very few outsiders are allowed to enter Bhutan; the Prince has long been intrigued by its unique and fiercely protected cultural heritage. Buddhism pervades all aspects of life and everything – from architecture to national costume to the national sport of archery – reflects a rich and complex tradition.

James Hart Dyke brought dual disciplines to his work on the royal tour: his training as an architect and as an artist. In England he specialises in country house 'portraits' in the tradition of Siberechts and Lambert, where the house is often set in a sweeping, dramatic landscape. Hart Dyke had met the Prince previously when he was working as a tutor for the Prince of Wales's Institute of Architecture summer schools in Sidon and Berlin. A lover of outdoor life, he was a natural choice for a trip which so spectacularly combined architecture and mountain landscape.

The Asian journey was planned by the artist with all the meticulousness of a Victorian explorer setting off for the Congo. His formal suit ('it seemed strange drawing in a suit') was made with a special pocket for his loose-leaf sketchbook. Pencil drawings were washed with watercolour at the end of long days. He took his treasured wooden carrying box, specially designed by his father, which houses half-a-dozen 15 x 30 cm painting boards and jars. Slung from a sturdy strap, it converts to a miniature 'easel' with pegs to hold the boards and holes for the jars. Such forethought served James well on treks up vertiginous Bhutani valleys in intense heat and thin Himalayan air. 'The Prince strode effortlessly upwards with the rest of us – staff and press – puffing in his wake', Hart Dyke laughs.

James Hart Dyke's instinctive feel for architecture is expressed in his oil sketches of Bhutan. The sloping white mass of the dzongs – monastery-fortresses perched on rocky outcrops – forms the focus of several paintings (Cat. 109, 111). Catching the light across a valley, they seem soaring, ethereal; close to, they have a massive power, conveyed in one of Hart Dyke's watercolours by the ant-like figures standing in the shadows.

The oil sketches were mostly completed in under an hour: 'I'm used to painting landscape; you have to work fast'. One dazzling example shows the path to the Tiger's Nest Monastery, the birthplace of Tantric Buddhism in Bhutan. Nearby, tall fluttering prayer flags point to the heavens at one of the highest spots on earth. For James, the prayer flags came to epitomise Bhutan. His on-the-spot sketch shows the slender flags white against a pale blue wash of sky. The Prince was painting nearby, equally transfixed.

The prayer flags form the subject of a large oil painting which

Hart Dyke started back in his Clerkenwell studio. Fluttering in the stiff breeze against a burnished blue Himalayan sky, they sum up the artist's philosophy of capturing the essence of an experience: 'whether it is a feeling, a building, a mood'. Very few Westerners will ever see Bhutan. By depicting this astonishing 'Kingdom of the Thunder Dragon', Hart Dyke adds one more thread to the tapestry of the Prince's tours.

NOTES

Unless otherwise stated, all quotations from HRH The Prince of Wales in this publication come from an interview by Susan Morris and John Sheeran with the Prince at Sandringham on Wednesday 18 March 1998.

1. Quoted in M. Howard, 'House of Tudor: (2) Henry VIII', *The Dictionary of Art* (1996), Vol. 31, p.414.
2. Quoted in J. Roberts, *Royal Artists* (1987), p.103.
3. Quoted in the Exhibition Guide, *The Queen's Pictures: Royal Collectors through the Centuries* (National Gallery 1991), p.2.
4. HRH The Prince of Wales, *HRH The Prince of Wales Watercolours* (1991), p.14.
5. Ibid.
6. Ibid.
7. Ibid., p.13.
8. Julian Halsby, *The Art of Diana Armfield* (1995), p.73.
9. HRH The Prince of Wales, *HRH The Prince of Wales Watercolours* (1991), p.78.
10. M. Warner, *Queen Victoria's Sketchbook* (1979), p.209.
11. HRH The Prince of Wales, *HRH The Prince of Wales Watercolours* (1991), p.15.

Fig. 15 HRH The Prince of Wales with the tour artists at the launch of *Young Artists' Britain: HRH The Prince of Wales's Young Artists' Award* and *Travels with the Prince* in April 1998

WATERCOLOURS

by His Royal Highness The Prince of Wales

Cat. 1 *View from Le Barroux, Provence* 1994

Cat. 2 *Provençale Landscape* 1994

Cat. 3 *Cypress Trees in Provence* 1995

Cat. 4 *Provençale Landscape (ii)* 1996

Cat. 5 *Provençale Evening in September* 1996

Cat. 6 *Provençale Landscape* 1996

Cat. 7 *Château Le Barroux, Provence (ii)* 1996

Cat. 8 *Provençale Landscape (i)* 1996

Cat. 9
Looking towards Invercauld from Ballochbuie (i)
1993

Cat. 10 *From Auchtavan towards Invercauld* 1995

Cat. 11 *Cairngorms from Glen Gelder, Balmoral* 1997

Cat. 12 *Spring Evening on Deeside, Balmoral* 1997

Cat. 13 *Ben Stack and Loch Stack, Sutherland* 1997

Cat. 14 *View from Birkhall, Balmoral* 1997

Cat. 15 *Scottish Scene, January (iv)* 1998

Cat. 16 *Scottish Scene (i)* 1997

Cat. 17 *Scottish Scene, January (v)* 1998

Cat. 20 *View from the Hotel, Christchurch, New Zealand* 1994

Cat. 21 *Corfu* 1995

Cat. 22 *Monastery of St John the Divine, Patmos* 1993

Cat. 23 *Monemvasia, Greece* 1994

Cat. 24 *Samothraki* 1994

Cat. 25 *Greek Landscape, Summer (x)* 1996

Cat. 26 *Island of Senfos* 1995

Cat. 27 *Greek Island Landscape, Fishing Boats* 1996

Cat. 28 *Greek Landscape, Summer (vii)* 1996

Cat. 29 *Greek Landscape, Summer (ix)* 1996

Cat. 30 *Greek Landscape, Summer (iv)* 1996

Cat. 31 *Greek Landscape, Summer (vi)* 1996

Cat. 32 *Greek Landscape, Summer (i)* 1996

Cat. 33 *Greek Landscape, Summer (ii)* 1996

Cat. 34 *Roumeli Mountains near Gorge of Samaria* 1995

Cat. 35 *Wadi Qaram from Sayq, Oman* 1995

Cat. 36 *Moru Kopjes, Serengeti Plains, Tanzania* 1997

Cat. 37 *Ngorongoro from Hugo Hill, Serengeti Plains, Tanzania* 1997

Cat. 38 *View towards Seronera Hills, Serengeti Plains, Tanzania* 1997

Cat. 39 *Rufiji River from Mbuyuni Camp, Selous Game Reserve, Tanzania (i)* 1997

Cat. 40 *Rufiji River, Selous Game Reserve, Tanzania* 1997

Cat. 41 *Seronera Hills at Sunset, Serengeti Plains, Tanzania* 1997

Cat. 42 *Rufiji River from Mbuyuni Camp, Selous Game Reserve, Tanzania (ii)* 1997

Cat. 43 *The Hüreli, Klosters, Switzerland (ii)* 1994

Cat. 44 *Above Klosters, Looking West, Other Side of Valley* 1994

Cat. 45 *From the Hotel, Klosters* 1995

Cat. 46 *View of Gotschna from Pany, Klosters* 1996

Cat. 47 *Landscape, Sandringham* 1995

Cat. 48 *Tetbury Church from Highgrove* 1996

Cat. 49 *Norfolk Landscape in January* 1997

Cat. 50 *View from Abbeystead, Lancashire* 1997

TOUR ARTISTS

by John Sheeran

John Ward

John Ward was born in Hereford in 1917 and studied at Hereford School of Arts and Crafts in 1932-36. He went on to the Royal College of Art, where he won the Drawing Prize, and left in 1939 to join the Royal Engineers. He returned to the RCA in 1946 and was given the Travelling Scholarship in 1947. He worked for *Vogue* magazine in 1948-52, was elected an ARA in 1956 and an RA in 1966. He was a member of the Executive Committee of the National Art Collections Fund in 1976-87, received an Hon. DLitt from the University of Kent in 1982 and was awarded a CBE in 1984. He served as a Trustee of the Royal Academy of Arts in 1985-93, but resigned as an Academician in 1997.

John Ward has exhibited regularly at the Royal Academy Summer Exhibition and has had one man exhibitions at leading London galleries, including Agnew's, Jeremy Maas and Hazlitt, Gooden & Fox. Retrospective exhibitions of his work were held at the Royal Museum and Art Gallery, Canterbury in 1987 and in 1997, and at Agnew's in 1990. He has a considerable reputation as a fine draughtsman and painter of portraits and conversation pieces. He has received numerous public and private commissions, including a portrait of HRH The Princess Royal for the National Portrait Gallery; a record of the auctioneers Christie's in its bicentenary year and a group portrait for the Dilettante Society. The artist has also illustrated many books, including Laurie Lee's *Cider with Rosie*, Joyce Grenfell's *Stately as a Galleon* and H.E. Bates's autobiography. He most recently exhibited views of Vienna, Venice, Rome, Paris and Chantilly at Hazlitt, Gooden & Fox in May 1998. He lives and has his studio near Ashford in Kent.

Cat. 54 *HMY Britannia* 1985

John Ward first met HRH The Prince of Wales at Balmoral in 1962, having been commissioned by Her Majesty The Queen to sketch the Royal Family's stay there. The Queen was so pleased with the results that she asked the artist back the following year. Ward's pictures of Balmoral range from drawings of the principal rooms, Crathie Church and shooting parties to scenes of family life. Through Sir Michael Adeane, the Queen's Private Secretary, who was himself a keen amateur watercolour painter and collector, Ward met Edward Adeane, his son, who as the Prince of Wales's Private Secretary took the Prince to see Ward's exhibition at the

Above: Cat. 52 *View from HMY Britannia* 1985

Right: Cat. 53 *View of Venice from HMY Britannia I* 1985

Maas Gallery. The Prince purchased a large watercolour of the interior of The House of Lords as viewed from the gallery, and shortly afterwards commissioned the artist to record his wedding at St Paul's Cathedral in 1981. The following year he was commissioned to paint the christening of Prince William. In both instances he worked entirely on the spot before, during and after the ceremony: 'There was no point in using photographs. I think that any scratch that is done on the day has something to it.'

Two years later, the Prince commissioned a portrait from John Ward of the Princess of Wales painted from life at Kensington Palace. He started a portrait of the Prince as a companion piece, but struggled over many months with the picture's composition and lighting, and abandoned it. It was while he was working on the two portraits that the Prince asked the artist to accompany him on an official tour to Italy in 1985.

The tour of Italy took place from 19 April to 5 May 1985. John Ward flew from London to Sicily and boarded *HMY Britannia* at the port of Catania when the tour was more than half way through. The Prince, on his first visit to Italy, had, in between his more official engagements, already enjoyed a cultural feast: seeing Leonardo da Vinci's *Last Supper* in Milan; the Pitti Palace, Duomo, Santa Croce and the Uffizi Gallery in Florence; and the Roman Forum, Pantheon, Vatican Museums and St Peter's Basilica in Rome (the visit included an audience for the Prince and Princess with the Pope). *HMY Britannia* then sailed for Venice, stopping on the way for brief visits to Syracuse for an archaeological tour and at Trani near Bari to view the cathedral. The Royal Yacht arrived in Venice in the early morning of Saturday 4 May off St Mark's Square, turned around in the Guidecca Canal, repassed St Mark's and berthed nearby at the Riva dei Sette Martiri.

'It was incredible sailing into Venice,' recalls John Ward, who knew the city well from previous visits. 'What was wonderful about being with the Prince was that doors were opened to bits of

Cat. 55 *View of Venice from HMY Britannia II* 1985

Cat. 51 *The Quarterdeck, HMY Britannia* 1985

Opposite: Cat. 56 *Illustrated Letter to HRH The Prince of Wales 1993*

Venice I had never seen before'. This included the interior of the Palazzo Contarini-Corfu owned by the Count and Countess Rocca, which faces out on to the Grand Canal. The tour party visited popular tourist sites such as St Mark's Basilica and the Doge's Palace, the Byzantine Basilica on the island of Torcello and San Giorgio Maggiore, where John Ward attended a service with the Prince early on Sunday morning. The small sketchbook the artist carried around with him everywhere records those details which caught his eye: the Princess receiving a cake; a performance at La Fenice; glass blowing at Murano; an ever-present security guard; the Venice skyline; and Beating the Retreat on the quayside shortly before the Royal Yacht set sail on the Sunday evening. The impression is of rapidly drawn and painted snapshots of the visit: 'I'd never any idea of the pressure on such visits. I was with one of the doctors, who said "When we move, we move fast, so for God's sake keep with us!" I was absolutely amazed'.

The frantic pace on land contrasted greatly with the haven of the Royal Yacht. During the voyage up the Adriatic Sea to Venice

John Ward had sketched life on board, both above and below deck while the Prince painted views from the yacht. Now in Venice on the verandah deck, away from the crowds, the Prince and Ward painted in every spare moment the stunning views all around them, determined to make the most of the unique vantage point they enjoyed for a weekend. Ward says: 'Venice is the architectural nude. Just as you go on drawing the nude forever – it is the most fabulous exercise – you go to Venice and you can draw and draw it forever. As a piece of engineering and as a piece of fancy, the world has no comparison'. Ward worked on a series of lively watercolours on buff paper with white highlights (Cat. 51, 52, 55). Energetic in line and loose in brushwork, these pictures were not intended as 'finished' pieces, but rather to capture the uniqueness of the moment and the sensation of actually being there. The Prince commented at the time: 'I have been picking up some very useful hints and new techniques, the best of which is the value of a piece of white chalk. It has revolutionised the whole exercise for me! The only trouble is that while I am rubbing out my second drawing effort of a particular subject John is already painting another picture altogether, having finished the subject I am doing long before!'[1]

John Ward remembers the Prince's extraordinary commitment: 'I was amazed at his ability to go on working when the temperature as far as I was concerned was extremely uncomfortable. His hands were blue with cold. Once he's attached to a thing he's like a terrier. He sticks it out and goes on. He has an amazing power of concentration. Most amateurs slosh away and stand back and look at it, and then it's cup of tea time. He's got a determination far beyond that!'

John Ward stayed on in Venice after the Prince left, and was joined by his wife for a few days before returning by train to London. He later took his portfolio to Kensington Palace to show the Prince, who chose a dozen watercolours. Most now hang together at Highgrove: a unique record of *HMY Britannia* and of a memorable visit to Venice; and ample evidence that taking an official artist on tour could reap fascinating rewards.

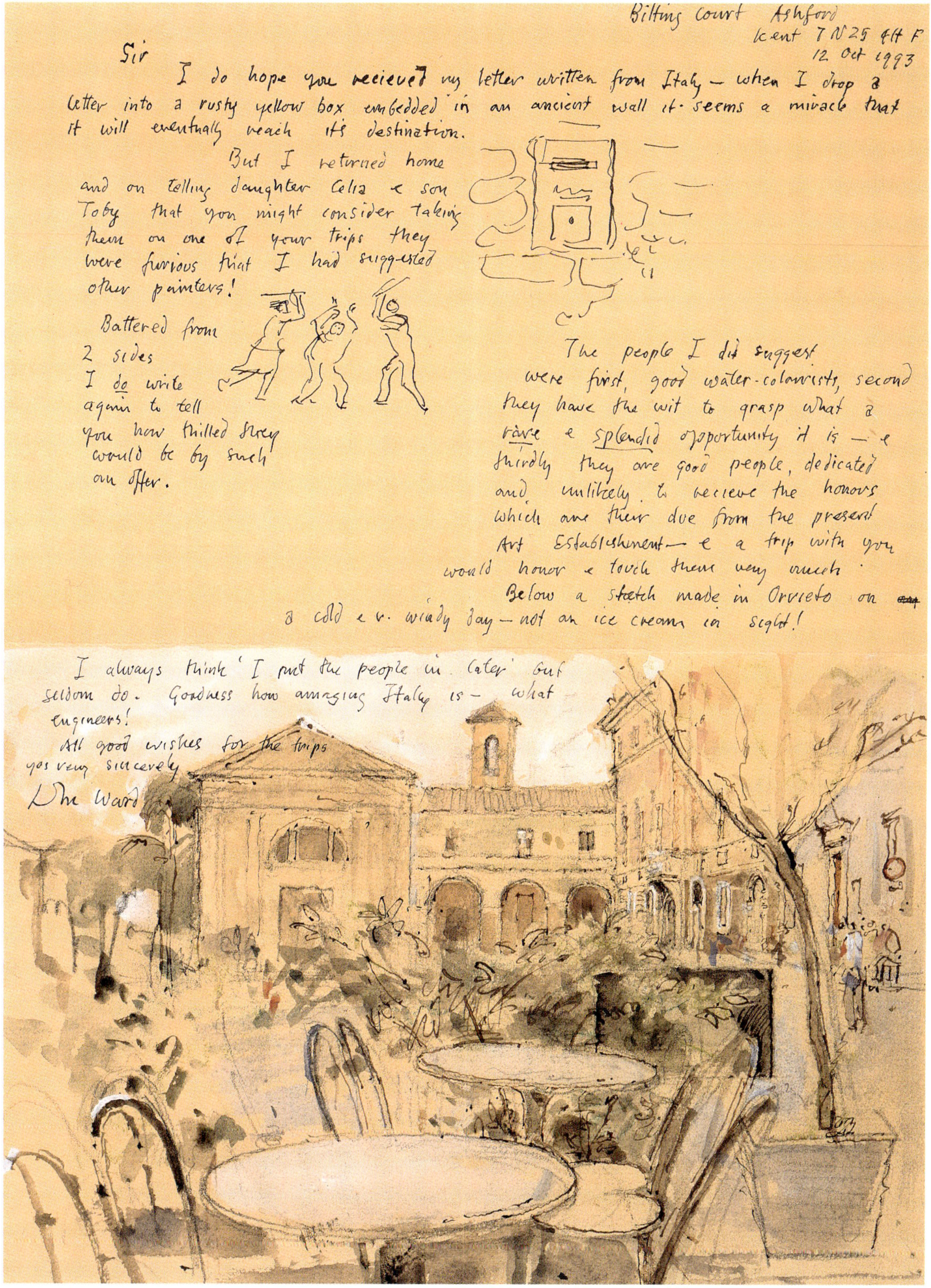
Bilting Court Ashford
Kent TN25 4HF
12 Oct 1993

Sir

I do hope you recieved my letter written from Italy – when I drop a letter into a rusty yellow box embedded in an ancient wall it seems a miracle that it will eventually reach its destination.

But I returned home and on telling daughter Celia & son Toby that you might consider taking them on one of your trips they were furious that I had suggested other painters!

Battered from 2 sides I do write again to tell you how thrilled they would be by such an offer.

The people I did suggest were first, good water-colourists, second they have the wit to grasp what a rare & splendid opportunity it is – & thirdly they are good people, dedicated and unlikely to recieve the honours which are their due from the present Art Establishment – & a trip with you would honor & touch them very much.

Below a sketch made in Orvieto on a cold & v. windy day – not an ice cream in sight!

I always think 'I put the people in later' but seldom do. Goodness how amazing Italy is – what engineers!

All good wishes for the trips

yours very sincerely

John Ward

Martin Yeoman

Martin Yeoman was born in 1953 in Surrey. On leaving school at 16 he first worked as a commercial artist. In 1973, he left work to travel to India and Pakistan, selling his drawings in order to survive. On returning to England in 1974, he set out to find an art school where he could learn more about drawing and painting. Seeking advice from the Royal Academy Schools, he took a portfolio of Indian drawings and showed them to Peter Greenham, who later that year invited him to be a guest student. In the autumn of 1975 he began a three-year course. Later, he was offered a fourth year, leaving the schools in 1979. He won the Silver Medal for Drawing, the David Murray Landscape Scholarship and the Richard Ford Scholarship, which enabled him to study in Madrid.

Martin Yeoman's work was first noticed and purchased by the collector Sir Brinsley Ford at the *Premiums* exhibition of 2nd Year students' work. Sir Brinsley has continued to acquire his work over the years and has introduced him to other collectors and patrons. In 1983, Martin Yeoman was given the opportunity to paint Basildon Park and Ashdown House, both National Trust properties, by Christopher Wall, then the Trust's historic buildings representative for the Thames and Chiltern Region. This led to numerous commissions from the National Trust's Foundation for Art, established in 1986 to encourage promising young artists to record properties, people and events associated with the Trust. A large retrospective exhibition of Yeoman's paintings, drawings, etchings and sculpture was organised by the Trust and shown at Mompesson House, Salisbury, in 1994.

Martin Yeoman has been on numerous painting trips abroad – Europe, the Middle East and the Far East – and is now well known for his travel pictures. He is also an accomplished portrait draughtsman and painter. His sitters have included Sir Alan Hodgkin, the Cambridge physiologist, in 1988 for the Order of Merit series in the Royal Collection; and the grandchildren of HM The Queen, commissioned in 1992 by the Royal Household as a gift to Her Majesty to mark the 40th anniversary of her reign, and exhibited together at the National Portrait Gallery in 1993. The artist lives and has his studio in Warminster.

Martin Yeoman was first introduced to HRH The Prince of Wales in early 1986 by Sir Brinsley Ford. The Prince looked through a portfolio of the artist's work and invited him on an official tour to the Gulf States. This took place from 10 to 21 November 1986 and covered Oman, Qatar, Bahrain and Saudi Arabia. The artist went loaded with sketchbooks and oils, but no watercolours. The tour party flew to Oman and boarded *HMY Britannia* at Mina

Cat. 61 *An Old Fort near Ra's Al Hadd, Oman* 1987

Qaboos, Muscat. As usual, the Royal Yacht was to be used as a base and for official entertainment. The first two days were taken up with formal engagements – an audience with the Sultan, a visit to the Oman Museum, lunches, receptions and dinners. Martin Yeoman recalls: 'I found staying within the confines of the tour a little limiting at first. However, what I found most rewarding was working within the tour group itself and drawing people going about their daily life outside it. By doing this, I felt I had the best of both worlds. I was able to see within a ruler's palace and also seek out dingy corners full of life in the souk. It was a remarkable experience to be able to move between one and the other'.

On one occasion, Martin Yeoman was sketching a man in the street sitting in a wheelbarrow. He was promptly arrested as the building behind turned out to be a police station. Yeoman was held on suspicion of being a spy but was soon released after his official security tag was noticed.

Late on the second day in the Gulf, *HMY Britannia* set sail for Ra's Al Hadd on the Omani coast, south of Muscat, arriving early the next morning. The artist remembers: 'In the afternoon, we spent a few hours on a beach next to a lagoon. The Prince headed up the beach to a fort on a small hill and came across some Omanis sitting in the shade of a tree. They thought the Prince and his party were English fishermen who had strayed into their seas. They were perplexed by this as the season was wrong. *HMY Britannia* was hidden out of sight by the headland. The Prince's party had a game of football with the village boys. The Prince went off to paint and I went back to the water's edge to paint a rough structure I had seen used for drying nets. It was an extraordinary day'. The scene has since provided the subject for numerous paintings and drawings. The Prince later recalled the day: 'I slunk off to settle myself into what I hoped was a relatively scorpion-free zone... The colours in that part of the world can be breathtaking. You would think it was all yellow ochre sand, but in the early mornings and evenings the rocky outcrops momentarily become flushed with orange, pink, purple and violet.'[2]

For the rest of the trip it was back to a full timetable. Martin Yeoman drew on the island of Masirah during a visit to an airforce

Cat. 60 *A Dow on the Lagoon at Ra's Al Hadd, Oman* 1987

Cat. 62 *A Camel Grinding Sesame Seeds, Sana', Yemen* 1987

base; sketched the Prince and Princess of Wales at an official state banquet given by the Amir of Qatar in the Rayyan Palace, Doha; painted dow building yards in Bahrain; drew portraits in Riyadh; and sketched at Musmak Fort and in the desert at Thumamah. When on the move, Yeoman dashed off vigorous pencil and crayon sketches; when he had time to stand still or sit, he worked delicately in ink or silverpoint using a carefully observed and descriptive line to capture the essential character of the subject. *HMY Britannia* was rejoined at Jeddah on Wednesday 19 November, after the group had toured the old city and visited a UK Saudi Trade Fair. The Royal Yacht then sailed up the Red Sea, through the Suez Canal to Cyprus, the Princess and her party disembarking at Hurghada on the Egyptian side to return to London.

On the yacht, Martin Yeoman turned to the crew as his subject matter and instantly won their respect as they witnessed his remarkable drawing skills in action. He drew the flag officer, Rear Admiral John Garnier, and the Chief Yeoman on the bridge of *HMY Britannia* as well as other members of the Prince's entourage, including the chefs and valets. His sketch of Coxswain Norris (Cat. 57), the longest serving member of the crew and known to all as 'Norrie', is a particular favourite of the Prince's and was much admired by the crew. (On his retirement in 1988 after 34 years service, Norrie was presented by the Duke of Edinburgh with a life size portrait of himself by Yeoman, commissioned as a gift by past and present Royal Yacht officers.) Yeoman entered into the spirit of life on board, even agreeing to go through the unique but terrifying experience of being hauled across from *HMY Britannia* to an accompanying frigate, *HMS Scylla*, while both were moving.

During the Gulf trip, Martin Yeoman formed a friendship with Stephen Day, head of the Middle East department of the Foreign Office, who had been acting as the Prince's adviser. He gave the artist invaluable advice on where to go and how to behave. At the end of the tour, Yeoman told the Prince that he wished he had more time to paint in the Gulf to do justice to the subject. The trip had fired his interest and imagination. At the Prince's request,

Right: Cat. 57 *Coxswain Norrie, HMY Britannia* 1986

Below: Cat. 59 *Blind Omani Fisherman, Ra's Al Hadd, Oman* 1987

Yeoman was able to return in 1987 with Stephen Day on a trip sponsored by Sheikh Khalifah of Qatar, visiting all the countries again, plus Yemen ('If you want to see the real Arabia', Stephen Day had commented, 'go to Yemen'). At the end of 1987, 33 oil paintings and 47 drawings were shown in an exhibition, *Two Arabian Tours of the Middle East by Martin Yeoman* at Agnew's, London. The artist returned to the Gulf twice more, in 1989 and in 1996, on the latter occasion to produce a series of etchings to illustrate Tim Mackintosh-Smith's book *Yemen: Travels in Dictionary Land.* The British Council organised an exhibition entitled *Yeoman's Yemen* the following year, which was shown at the National Art Gallery in Sana'. The Prince was delighted that his second official tour artist had benefited so much in the long term from his original trip to the Gulf and that such a strong cultural bridge with the Gulf had been established. In 1997, he invited the artist and Tim Mackintosh-Smith to Highgrove to discuss their impressions of Yemen and purchased two of Yeoman's etchings of the country to add to his impressive collection of the artist's work.

Martin Yeoman joined two further official tours: Hong Kong in November 1989, and India and Nepal in February 1992. Neither was as rewarding artistically for him as the Gulf tour. He flew out to Hong Kong as the Prince was coming to the end of the tour and boarded *HMY Britannia* shortly before it sailed to the New Territories. It was a quiet trip, with Yeoman painting alongside the Prince and instructing him on various techniques, such as painting in watercolour on a toned ground. The Prince later purchased one of the artist's oil studies showing the forms of the islands dissolving in the haze. The Prince made the most of his time off, ending the day painting watercolours of the disappearing light in Double Haven Bay. He later wrote: 'There was a beautiful sunset over the distant Chinese hills and the White Ensign was flapping gently to and fro in the soft breeze. The whole scene was gloriously peaceful and I found it impossible to resist the urge to capture this atmosphere'.[3]

The tour to India and Nepal had a much tighter schedule of flights and visits : Delhi, Agra, Jaipur, Hyderabad, Bangalore, Calcutta and on to Kathmandu in six days. 'For the first two

days', recalls the artist, 'I had difficulty as my sleep pattern had gone awry. Sadly, I missed several unique opportunities; notably drawing the President's Guard which was arranged for me'. By the time the party reached Jaipur and Hyderabad, Martin Yeoman decided the best approach would be to work from a car: 'I had memories of nearly 20 years before of large excitable crowds forming in front of wherever I decided to work. In the car I was able to have my sketchbooks, ink and watercolour laid out beside me, stop when I saw something I wanted to draw and move on before too many people noticed'.

The second day, Yeoman flew with the Princess to Agra to see the Taj Mahal. Overwhelmed by the setting and the grounds, he strayed from the official party out of the security cordon, a cardinal error for a tour artist, only to find the police would not let him back in. The following day was a highlight of the trip for Yeoman. Flying to Jaipur, he took a car a few miles to the Amber Palace, an outstanding example of Rajput architecture set in a beautiful hillside location overlooking a lake which reflected its ramparts and terraces. Another lasting impression of the tour for the artist was trekking with the Prince's party in the shadow of the Annapurna range (Cat. 63): 'Once in the rhythm of walking, stopping and drawing, I found a greater harmony with myself and my work'.

Cat. 58 *Head Study of Gardener, British Council, Bahrain* 1987

Cat. 63 *The Annapurna Range, Himalayas* 1992

Derek Hill

Derek Hill was born in Southampton in 1916 and started his career as a stage designer, studying in Munich, Paris, Vienna, and the former Soviet Union in the early 1930s. He started to paint seriously in 1938 in Paris, where he set up his first studio. The Contemporary Art Society purchased one of his works in 1940 and he was given his first one man exhibition in 1943. He has had numerous exhibitions since, including retrospective shows at the Whitechapel Art Gallery in 1961, Christie's in 1992, Colnaghi in 1994 and UNESCO Paris in 1997. He himself has also organised exhibitions, including Degas at the Edinburgh Festival and the Tate Gallery in 1952, and Landseer at the Royal Academy in 1961. Twice appointed Art Director of the British School in Rome in the 1950s, he has written for the *Times Literary Supplement, Burlington Magazine, Observer* and *Spectator*, and produced books on Islamic art. Since the early 1950s, he has lived in Hampstead and Donegal and travelled and painted extensively. He was instrumental in setting up the National Trust's Foundation for Art and has given the Trust his collection

Cat. 64 *Tory Island: West to the Lighthouse* 1975

of French pictures, including works by Degas, Redon, and Seurat, which is displayed at Mottisfont Abbey in Hampshire. Best known as a painter of portraits, his numerous sitters have included John Betjeman, Kenneth Clark, Noel Coward, Lord Hailsham, Yehudi Menuhin, Lord Mountbatten, Lord Olivier and Michael Tippett. He is also an accomplished landscape painter, some of his most successful works being small oil on panel paintings of Donegal, and Tory Island where he has a painting hut and paints throughout the seasons.

Derek Hill first met HRH The Prince of Wales in 1971 when he was commissioned to paint a portrait of him by Trinity College, Cambridge, where the Prince was a student. A friend for many years of HM The Queen Mother and Lord Mountbatten, Derek Hill is also one of the Prince's closest artist mentors and friends. He has encouraged the Prince's own painting and stimulated a wide appreciation of art, especially Islamic architecture and design. A frequent travelling companion of the Prince, he has stayed with him to paint at Balmoral, Sandringham and Highgrove. Over the years, the Prince has acquired a group of mostly small landscape paintings done on the spot by the artist, either on Tory Island or during his travels with him. These include *Tory Island: West to the Lighthouse* 1975 (Cat. 64), which shows a favourite coastal view in the early evening light. As with most of his paintings in recent years, it is painted on a Cuban cigar box lid and is characterised by minimal painterly means, a particular atmospheric effect of time and place and an impressive sense of scale and grandeur for such a small work. The limited palette, muted colours, feeling of light breaking out, and the silvery sheen as it hits the sea, are handled by a painter who clearly understands the performance of this landscape at different times of year and day, known intimately through decades of close observation. These are all qualities which the Prince greatly admires, and though Derek Hill has never taught him painting techniques, the Prince has benefited from studying his example.

Cat. 65 *St Nicolas Island, Fethiye, Turkey* 1989

In his painting, *Kalahari* 1991 (Cat. 67), also owned by the Prince, Derek Hill shows that the artist has opportunities through studying and even reinterpreting the work of others. The small oil is his own version of a Kalahari landscape watercolour painted by the Prince; the mentor using the amateur's work to make the point. The painting typifies Hill's working method of carefully controlled but energetic brushwork, and a layered and worn texture in which the colour and material of the panel showing through, plays an important part. The abstract and figurative elements are equally suggestive: forms, shifting light and changing colours are conjured from the imagination and skillfully handled.

Derek Hill first accompanied the Prince abroad during the royal tour to Turkey in 1989 from 11 to 20 May, which combined official visits and trips to ancient sites, such as Bodrum and Ephesus, with a private holiday for sailing and painting. Unlike other tour artists, he did not accompany the Prince on official engagements and

Cat. 66 *Le Jardin de Monet, Giverny* 1990

paint aspects of the tour. He knew Turkey extremely well, having first visited the country with Dame Freya Stark in 1954, and again in 1958 to start a photographic survey of early Islamic architecture. He was thus uniquely placed to tell the Prince about the country and its ancient culture and to advise on picturesque views to paint.

One evening the Prince and Hill painted together on the island of St Nicolas near Fethiye on the southwestern Turkish coast: 'Rarely have I witnessed a more romantic sunset than this one...', the Prince recalled. 'Trying to capture its transitory translucence was beyond me... but the desire to get out my paint box and to crouch amongst the painful rocks of a Turkish island was overwhelming'.[4] Derek Hill's modest oil (Cat. 65) finely balances the spectacle of the sun setting and the column of light reflected in the sea, with the stillness and quiet of a timeless scene. The impact of dying light on huge coastal forms provides a contrast: one in shadow and bold; the other in a state of metamorphosis from hazy dissolved features to strong outline and heavy body.

A similar painting subject occurs in Derek Hill's *Château Le Barroux* 1996 (Cat. 69), in which the dramatic setting of a castle in Provence is captured at sunset. It was painted in one session, during a private holiday with the Prince. The challenge for the artist was to render the effects of the light on different elements of the composition: the still bright fields in the foreground, and the hill in half light, silhouetted against the hazy glare in the sky. It is also a favourite scene of the Prince, who has spent many hours with Derek Hill painting it during private visits to the area in recent years (Cat. 7). Nearby are the Dentelles, a line of rugged hills which

Cat. 67 *Kalahari* 1991

Cat. 68 *County Mayo* 1995

stretch into the distance, which have made an equally demanding and rewarding subject-matter for the two of them (Cat. 70).

On 4 June 1990, Derek Hill and the Prince privately visited Monet's house and gardens at Giverny. After a brief tour of the gardens, they had an informal lunch in Monet's dining room using Monet's cutlery and plates. In the afternoon the Prince and the artist settled down to paint. The session was a unique experience for Derek Hill and resulted in one of his favourite paintings (Cat. 66). He remembers the Prince being unable to finish his before it was time to leave, a common frustration for him.

Another memorable painting trip for Derek Hill occurred immediately after the Prince's official visit to the Republic of Ireland on 31 May and 1 June 1995. The Prince had had an exhausting schedule, which included a tour of the Irish Government buildings, a dinner at Dublin Castle, visits to the Mansion House, a community care centre, the British Tourist Authority offices and Trinity College (where he viewed the Book of Kells in the Library), followed by a private lunch with the President, Mary Robinson, and trips to the Newgrange Megalithic Tomb and Butterstream Gardens, Trim. Afterwards, Hill joined the Prince and friends for a walking, fishing and painting break in County Mayo on the West coast. He was very familiar with the landscape, which he first visited in 1946 when he spent the year painting in Galway, Mayo and on Achill Island.

The Prince's party stayed at the Lodge at Delphi, on the southern end of Doo Lough, and were advised by staff there where to go for the most spectacular views of mountains and lakes. The Prince and Derek Hill were determined to get out and paint, whatever the weather. Hill's painting *County Mayo* (Cat. 68) records the stunning scenery as well as the clouds closing in. He remembers: 'It was painted on a very wet day. We sat together to paint the view when soon after the rain came pouring down. The Prince gave me the watercolour he had done as a present. It was almost pointillist, it had spots of rain all over it!'

From 23 to 27 February 1996, the Prince went on an official visit to Morocco, accompanied by the Islamic art expert Keith Critchlow and Derek Hill. The tour started with a weekend of visits to historical sites of great interest – the Ksar Air Ben Haddou, the Kasbah of Telouet, various buildings and gardens in Marrakesh, and the Ksour of the Tafilalet. Monday 26 February was given over to a military display, a visit to a hospital cardiac unit and a dinner with the Crown Prince; Tuesday morning was taken up with to a visit to Al Akhawayn University and the afternoon with a tour of the remarkable Roman ruins at Volubilis, near Fes. There were slots earmarked in the intensely busy schedule 'for painting', at the Kawwiya Ksar and at Volubilis, but when it came to it, there was too little time and Derek Hill did no painting at all. The Prince, however, managed a painting of palm trees in the desert, the first time he had tackled the subject.

Cat. 69 *Château Le Barroux* 1996

Cat. 70 *Towards the Dentelles, Le Barroux* 1996

Peter Kuhfeld

Peter Kuhfeld was born in Cheltenham in 1952, studied at Leicester Polytechnic in 1972-76, and then taught drawing and painting at Rugby School of Art for two years. While teaching, he showed his work to Peter Greenham, the Keeper of the Royal Academy Schools and was invited to study there in 1977-80. He was taught by Greenham, Norman Blamey and Jane Dowling, later winning the David Murray Landscape Prize, the Royal Academy of Arts Silver Medal for Drawing, the Royal College of Surgeons Dooley Prize for Anatomical Drawing, the Elizabeth Greenfield Foundation Scholarship and the Richard Ford Scholarship to Spain. His first one-man exhibition was held at the Highgate Gallery, London in 1983 and he has since exhibited at major London commercial galleries, including Agnew's and W.H.Patterson. His work has been shown in exhibitions organised by the National Trust Foundation for Art, such as *The Long Perspective* in 1987, *Salute to Turner* in 1989 and *The Broad Horizon* in 1990, and the National Trust's Centenary exhibition at Christie's in 1995. He was elected a member of the New English Art Club in 1986 and of the Royal Society of Portrait Painters in 1992. He is a supporter of the *Venice in Peril* shows at W.H.Patterson. In 1992 he was commissioned by HM The Queen to draw a portrait of Yehudi Menuhin for the Order of Merit series in the Royal Collection. His work has also been included in the *Discerning Eye* exhibitions at the Mall Galleries. He lives and works in Kent.

Cat. 73 *Young Girl in a Blue Dress, Umuagbai Village, Nigeria* 1990

Like Martin Yeoman, his fellow student at the Royal Academy Schools, Peter Kuhfeld's work was recommended to HRH The Prince of Wales by Sir Brinsley Ford, who had purchased a number of his student drawings. Sir Brinsley showed the Prince a selection of his work, including a sensitive portrait of the artist's daughter, Jemimah, which the Prince purchased. In 1988, a commission from the Prince followed to paint separate portraits from life of the Princes William and Harry in the private apartments at Kensington Palace. These and related drawings now hang at Highgrove.

Early in 1990 the Prince's Office at St James's Palace called asking the artist to accompany the Prince and Princess on an official tour to Africa from 15 to 26 March. Peter Kuhfeld, though widely

Cat. 72 *On the Road to Umuagbai Village, Rivers State, Nigeria* 1990

Opposite: Cat. 71 *The Durbar at Maiduguri, Nigeria* 1990

travelled in Europe, had never been to the African continent before. The tour would take him first to Nigeria, then Cameroon and finally for a less formal stay in Tunisia. He flew to Lagos with the rest of the tour party: 'I took practically my entire studio to cover every eventuality'. On boarding *HMY Britannia* in Lagos marina, Rear Admiral Sir John Garnier offered the use of his map room to the artist as a makeshift studio but Kuhfeld set one up in his cabin, not wanting to be an inconvenience. He decided to shadow the Prince all day, every day, if he could keep to the pace: sketching and making notes during the day and painting in his cabin at night, without using any photographs as aids. He recalls: 'It was a nightmarish pace. We were flying all over Nigeria, to and from Lagos. From my point of view it was marvellous because it gave me, in a comparatively short period, pictures of the country with its extraordinary landscapes, from green, lush river states in the south, to rainforest in the central region, and savanna in the north. The other thing I learnt was that I needed to draw at quite a pace'.

On the third day of the tour, Saturday 17 March 1990, Peter Kuhfeld set off with the rest of the party by plane for a day in Maiduguri in the far east state of Borno, near Lake Chad. After a lunch at the state governor's house, a visit to the Shehu of Bornu in his palace, and a trip to a leprosy hospital and a rehabilitation village, the Prince, Princess and their party took their seats in the late afternoon in front of the Shehu's palace for a durbar. The Prince was keen that Kuhfeld had a good viewpoint. 'I clambered up to the top of the temporary stand. The sight of waves of colourful mounted tribesman, accompanied by dancers and musicians, amid clouds of dust in the pinkish afternoon light, riding past to pay homage to the Prince and Princess who were sitting in a tented area, was an unforgettable experience. It was almost as old as time and so profound', he recalls. 'It must have been extremely moving for the Prince and Princess. It certainly was for me. It was so vast – a similar grandeur to that of *Lawrence of Arabia.* I did tiny drawings of the figures in the foreground which led naturally into the whole composition. I could see how the format of the picture might be developed from that point' (Cat. 71).

Towards the end of the tour to Nigeria, the party stayed in Port Harcourt in the Rivers State, enjoying a cultural evening presented by the military governor in his residence. Peter Kuhfeld painted an oil painting of it from a wooden gallery, looking down. He found that years toiling over the depiction of the human figure in movement from all angles, now served him well for drawing or painting a scene instantaneously. He had trained himself to look clearly and carefully, and memorise certain details of visual information at a glance. The next day, the last in Nigeria, Kuhfeld was driven with the tour group to Umuagbai village to visit a new weaving centre for rural women and to walk around the village farm. The artist was captivated by the fresh faced beauty of the children running around excitedly, in particular a girl wearing a

Cat. 74 *Tamanrasset, Algeria* 1990

brilliant blue dress who came up to him to look inquisitively, a moment movingly portrayed shortly afterwards by the artist (Cat. 73). On the drive, families waited by the roadside for a glimpse of the visitors: 'An awful lot of people had never seen a white man before. So as we went past, I noticed people just staring, not quite sure who or what they were staring at. I was in a Land Rover which slowed down just long enough for me to take it in. I painted a picture of this on the Royal Yacht later in the day' (Cat. 72).

Shortly before leaving Port Harcourt to return to Lagos and rejoin *HMY Britannia* for the next leg of the tour, the party was entertained with a traditional regatta with war canoes, musicians and dancers. For Kuhfeld, it was another amazing spectacle which he did drawings of and painted later. There was, indeed, so much painting for him to catch up on, that he went to see the Prince to say he would prefer to complete what he could of the Nigeria paintings in his cabin and not do any painting in Cameroon. The Prince was well aware how frustrating it was not to be able to finish pictures through lack of time, and sympathised. Kuhfeld stuck to his plan not to take on new painting subjects in Cameroon, but the tour schedule was so enticing that he found it hard to confine himself to his naval studio. The second day provided him with one of the most memorable experiences of the tour – flying over the rainforest in a helicopter with the Prince in the company of Mark Bovey from Kew Gardens: 'The image that I saw as we flew over the top of the rainforest will never leave me'.

Peter Kuhfeld showed his paintings at intervals to the Prince, usually late in the afternoon over tea and discussed their progress. The next stage of the tour to Tunisia was low key. Most of the party, including the Princess, had returned to London after Cameroon. Kuhfeld flew with the Prince to Tunis on Friday 23 March in a Hercules transport plane, stopping off for half an hour to refuel at Tamanrasset in the Sahara. He remembers: 'I was invited by the captain into the cockpit. Flying low over the Sahara was a tremendous sensation. We all got out of the plane at Tamanrasset and walked into the desert. I just did a very quick drawing with colour notes of the emptiness in front of me and then did a painting at a later date. I had never done anything like a desert landscape before' (Cat. 74).

Up until this time on the tour, it had been far too hot to do any painting outside. However, the climate in Tunis was more comfortable. A trip was arranged during the weekend to the ancient Roman city of Thugga (modern day Dougga), famous for its Hellenistic mausoleum built in the 2nd century BC in honour of a Numidian prince, and for its remarkably well preserved forum, temples, theatre, villas and baths. The Prince chose to paint a view, while Kuhfeld immediately painted the Capitol, a beautifully proportioned classical building (Cat. 75): 'It was rather disconcerting to stand painting in ruins when you had a guy with a Kalashnikov rifle a few yards away from you!' After returning to Tunis, the artist showed all his paintings from the tour to the British Ambassador, Stephen Day, in whose residence the Prince was staying. He was invited back by the Ambassador the following year as a guest to paint in Tunis and elsewhere, but that time, his visit coincided with the Gulf War and he was advised not to travel.

Just eight months after the long African tour, Peter Kuhfeld was bound for Japan, accompanying the Prince primarily to record the coronation of the 125th Emperor, Akihito, in the Imperial Palace in Tokyo on Monday 12 November. The tour party flew into Haneda Airport in the afternoon of Saturday 10 November to face a feverish reception from the media, the like of which the artist had never experienced: 'When we arrived and got off the plane, the number of photographers was unbelievable. We couldn't see for the banks of flashlights. It was extraordinary. The centre of Tokyo was closed off. I've never seen such security. The world's dignitaries were flying in and there were paramilitary police

Cat. 75 *The Capitol at Dougga, Tunisia* 1990

everywhere. I had this horrible feeling that I wouldn't even get close to the ceremony of enthronement!' The next day was Remembrance Sunday and Kuhfeld attended a ceremony with the Prince at the Commonwealth war cemetery at Hodogoya.

That afternoon they visited the exquisite Japanese garden, wooden buildings and ceramics collection of the privately owned Hatakeyama Museum. Before the Prince and Princess and party had a lunch hosted by the owner in the Hannya-En restaurant, Kuhfeld looked around. He said to the Prince afterwards that he would like to return to paint one room in particular to record its quiet simplicity and calming atmosphere. The Prince arranged for him to go the following morning and the artist spent a peaceful few hours sitting on the floor, painting, interrupted only briefly by armed security guards protecting another dignitary who was being entertained there. Two days later, Kuhfeld gave the finished painting (Cat. 76) to the Prince as a 42nd birthday present: 'He's passionate about painting and this little picture was in a sense the antithesis of the pace of the official engagements he was involved in. It was an interior that might enable him to remember a quiet moment in a bustling, and at times frantic world. I remember talking to him in Tunis about the reasons behind him taking different painters on these trips. It was very interesting, because he said he wanted to give them the opportunity to see parts of the world and paint what they saw. His role, I felt, was to allow people and places to connect. I think it is a marvellous idea'.

Unfortunately, as Kuhfeld feared, it was impossible to get a good view of the Emperor's coronation the following day. The ceremony took place a long way from where the guests were assembled. Kuhfeld was especially interested in the court costumes and wanted to paint a picture of the Empress in her kimono: 'I did manage a sketch of the Emperor, but it was like looking down the wrong end of a telescope. Afterwards, I tried to develop the image further as an oil sketch, but said to the Prince it wasn't going to work and so it was left unfinished'.

Kuhfeld decided to get out of Tokyo the following day and was kindly taken by an embassy official to a wooden gateway shrine out at sea, a couple of hours drive from the city. His companion was astonished when Kuhfeld said he would need to get much closer to the gateway. A boat would be needed, but they ran out of time. He soon abandoned the idea and instead produced a detailed drawing of a hillside temple nearby.

In 1993, Peter Kuhfeld again accompanied the Prince on a tour, this time as part of a small team visiting Poland from 17 to 20 May. The visit started in Warsaw, and was packed with engagements: laying a wreath at the tomb of the Unknown Soldier; meeting President Lech Walesa at the Belweder Palace; a review of a teaching project at the British Council; a reception hosted by the British Ambassador followed by a tour of the Royal Castle; a state dinner in the Wilanow Palace; a meeting at the Council of Ministers; an address to students at Warsaw University; and a reception for British businessmen and the Chamber of Commerce. Kuhfeld likened it to 'a series of hit and runs', which made it difficult to stay in any one place long enough to paint.

The tour moved on after a day and a half to Gdansk, where the artist saw the Shipyard Memorial, the Gdansk Renaissance Theatre, and walked through the Old Town. His prime interest was in the mixture of styles of Polish architecture and the restoration

Cat. 76 *Morning in the Hatakeyama, Tokyo* 1990

of old buildings. The country seemed like a cultural crossroads of Europe, between east and west, north and south. He sketched everywhere he went: a cathedral with an interior like something in a Dutch 17th century painting; a piece of Baroque flamboyance on the edge of the Warsaw Ghetto; and the imposing structure of a town hall. In Krakow the next day, Kuhfeld visited Wawel Castle and the Cathedral alongside, as well as the Town Hall, Cloth Hall and Church of St Mary. Later back in England, he produced a series of oil paintings showing buildings in the the three cities which had caught his attention (Cat. 77).

There was, however, a complex of buildings visited on the last day of the tour which Kuhfeld found deeply disturbing and impossible to paint: 'We went to the Majdanek concentration camp in the east of Poland, near the Russian border. It was immediately horrifying. It's still standing with its contents. We saw the crematorium and the mass execution ditches. That was terrible, really terrible. It showed humanity the process of slaughter. I remember the chimney for the ovens. I did a drawing of that and the different flags that flew when different communities were being led to death. Walking through the site was profound. I said to the Prince 'I'm sorry, I can't come up with anything'. He understood. He said 'I know what you mean'. There was just no single image or too many images to capture the horror. You had to witness the shadows of humanity walking to their deaths'.

Looking back, Peter Kuhfeld regards the support of the Prince of Wales as a catalyst for his development as an artist: 'The trips I went on have had a substantial impact on my work. It enabled me to see other things and experience people and places. The Prince understands painters and wants them to experience the profundity of the world. The important thing is that he continues to give painters the opportunities that these tours provide, doors that would not normally be opened. He has helped me in other things I have wanted to do, always with a generosity and understanding that makes him such an outstanding patron'.

Cat. 77 *Town Hall, Gdansk, Poland* 1993

John Sergeant

Cat. 78 *Illustrated Letter to HRH The Prince of Wales* 1990

John Sergeant was born in London in 1937 and studied at Canterbury College of Art in 1954-57, with a break for National Service in 1957-59, continuing his studies at the Royal Academy Schools in 1959-62, where he won the Drawing Prize in his final year. From 1962-69 he taught at Canterbury College of Art and Dover and Folkestone Schools of Art, and also carried out his own commissioned work as well as working as an occasional studio assistant to the artist John Ward. His work as a book illustrator has included *Oliver Twist* and Richard Church's *Portrait of Canterbury.* In 1981, inspired by the *Interiors* exhibition at Hazlitt, Gooden & Fox, London, he began two years' of drawing and painting commissions of country house interiors including Castle Coole, Stowell Park and Deene Park. Sergeant moved to Wales in 1983 and has since held one man shows in London: during the late 1980s and early 1990s with the Maas Gallery, and more recently with Hazlitt, Gooden & Fox. He has exhibited with the Royal Society of Portrait Painters, at the Victoria and Albert Museum, the New Grafton Gallery and in the Royal Academy Summer Exhibition. His work is represented in the Royal Library, Windsor, and the Fitzwilliam Museum, Cambridge, and he is best known for his still life drawings. He lives and has his studio in Powys.

HRH The Prince of Wales first noticed John Sergeant's drawings at the National Trust exhibition *The Long Perspective* at Agnew's in 1987, in which the artist showed drawings and watercolours of Erddig House in Wales. The Prince asked him to do some drawings for his book *A Vision of Britain* in 1989 and invited him to stay at Sandringham the following year to make a record of several large barns on the estate. Sergeant recalls: 'The Prince clearly realised how important such buildings are in the landscape – they meant much to him'.[5]

The visit to Prague by the Prince and Princess of Wales, which John Sergeant accompanied, took place from 6 to 10 May 1991. Apart from the official meetings and functions including the Business Leaders Forum and Business in the Community, the focus for the trip was architectural heritage. Prague is a city rich in architectural treasures from the Romanesque period to the Neoclassical and Art Nouveau, and it has retained a rare architectural harmony. The Prince was keen to see and learn as much as possible,

Cat. 79 *Prague Skyline, Sv. Mikulas, Mala Strana* 1991

Cat. 80 *Prague: Hradcany* 1991

including the problems faced by the country's major cities. He opened the Civic Forum Foundation exhibition on endangered historical monuments at Charles University; attended a World Monuments Fund seminar; and toured castles, museums, town halls and squares in Prague, Bratislava and Brno, viewing restoration projects and environmental damage. Two years later, in 1993, the Prince established the Prague Heritage Fund to support restoration work in the Czech capital.

John Sergeant's brief was to reflect the visit in whatever way he felt he could. As were all the Prince's tour artists, he was bewildered at first, and amazed throughout by the sheer efficiency of the visit. The pace, however, was too fast and not conducive to sitting quietly and drawing, as he was accustomed to doing in his studio in rural Wales. He stayed with the Prince's entourage as it rushed around, making thumbnail sketches along the way, and then at quieter moments he returned to draw the places he had particularly noted. To do this uninterrupted, he got up each day at 5.30 am and worked for two or three hours before breakfast: 'I drew the obvious – it was all around one, a breathtakingly beautiful city. But I felt an unreality pervading, a Disney backdrop feel which concerned me, not for that moment but I feared for its future. Tourism when over and above a certain limit can for me, kill a place stone dead'.

The Prince's apartment was in Prague Castle and on arrival the Prince had taken Sergeant to see the superb views from his window, looking down over the city: 'The Prince was spellbound by its magnificence'. On the first morning, Sergeant was accompanied by a helpful and knowledgeable guide, who took him to a spot where the view was similar to that from the Castle and he sat down to record it in a double page image in his sketchbook (Cat. 79). The picture shows a panorama of Prague in which the city emerges in the early morning mist as the light begins to pick out the features of buildings which penetrate through the blanket of haze. The sharp sunlight illuminates the Baroque dome of St Nicholas church, the boldest passage of the composition, while delicate washes, deft touches of drawn line and a subtle use of the buff paper beautifully suggest atmosphere and distance. John Sergeant later sketched a view from the Vltava river looking up to the Castle and the Prince's quarters (Cat. 80), achieving a striking clarity of light and delineation of form with an economy of means. In a study of Charles Bridge (Cat. 81), which the Prince visited during the first afternoon, the brushwork is loose and the ink drawing energetic. The pictures reveal a strong interest in design, an interesting balance of the figurative and abstract possibilities of the cityscape and a telling reduction of a scene to its barest essentials, all of which result from intense concentration and observation.

John Sergeant reflects on the impact of the Prague visit: 'I don't think that it affected my work, it was all too brief, but it did make me realise that to be able to do justice to such work one needs to be trained to draw "on the hoof". Such skills have been lost, I believe'. He also believes that, as a supporter of the arts and artists, the Prince of Wales is an excellent role model: 'A good patron will, by his or her attitude, get the best from the artist. The Prince is concerned that one is comfortable and has all one needs. In my experience, he only *indicates* what he would like done and then leaves one to get on with it, never interfering. At the same time he is sympathetic, enthusiastic and encouraging. He is fascinated too by the technical side of painting and drawing and most appreciative of one's efforts. As a supporter, he always tries to get along to my exhibitions (quietly)!'

Cat. 81 *Charles Bridge, Prague* 1991

Toby Ward

Toby Ward was born in 1965 and in 1984 became a studio assistant to his father, the painter John Ward, who taught him to draw. He entered the Royal Military Academy at Sandhurst in 1986 and was commissioned into the Royal Welch Fusiliers, serving as an officer in Northern Ireland, Wales, Nepal, Canada, Malaysia and Germany. Throughout his time in the army he sketched his soldiers, the barracks and the countries they visited, and toured museums, galleries and exhibitions when off duty. He left the army in 1992 to study for a diploma in fine art and painting at the City & Guilds of London Art School in Kennington, determined to be a painter and illustrator. Toby Ward was commissioned in 1994 by the National Trust to make a series of drawings recording the restoration and conservation over three years of Chastleton House, Oxfordshire. He worked in Bosnia in 1995 with UN troops to record aspects of their life in the peace-keeping force and produced pictures of Burgundy and the Vosges region for the French Tourist Board. Sir Brinsley Ford also commissioned him to paint scenes from his life. Since graduating in 1996, Ward has worked on many illustration projects. In 1997, he returned to Bosnia to sketch the Royal Artillery and travelled to Drawsko in Poland to draw the First Armoured Division in the first military exercises by British troops on Warsaw Pact land. He worked at the Royal Opera House in summer 1997 to record aspects before its closure for modernisation and is making drawings of the rebuilding. He is also becoming established as a portrait painter. He lives and has his studio in East Sussex.

Toby Ward received a phone call from St James's Palace on the evening of Friday 5 November 1993 as he was preparing to go out to a Guy Fawkes bonfire night in Battersea Park. He was asked if he was able to accompany HRH The Prince of Wales on a tour to Saudi Arabia, Kuwait, the United Arab Emirates and Jordan, starting two days later. There had been a hitch as an artist had had to pull out at the last moment. Used to being called upon at short notice in the army, Ward accepted immediately. He knew a little about the Prince's tours through his father, who had been the official

Cat. 85 *Film Crew, Qurain Houses, Kuwait* 1993

Opposite top: Cat. 82
Sketchbook from the Gulf (i) 1993: *Dimbleby Interview on top of the Dunes, The Empty Quarter*

Opposite bottom: Cat. 83
Sketchbook from the Gulf (ii) 1993: *Lunch Given by The Amir of Kuwait* and *Visit to the Qurain Houses*

Lunch given by the Amir of Kuwait in a huge room that looked like a big top with the biggest chandelier suspended from the top in the centre.
I sat next to the retired head of the National bank.
In retirement he had set up the Kuwait Zoo – most of which had been destroyed by Iraqi troops.
He owned a house in Esher and was very fond of English apples

For pudding chocolate Big Bens were served at every table. 1.50pm A visit to the Quarain house where a Kuwaiti family held out against the invaders. The place was all but destroyed. There was just room to walk amongst the rubble.

Cat. 84 *The Qurain Houses, Kuwait* 1993

Opposite top: Cat. 86 *The Empty Quarter* 1993

Opposite bottom: Cat. 87 *Petra* 1993

artist to Italy in 1985: 'Instead of going out to the cinema on the Sunday night I was stepping off a plane on to a red carpet in Riyadh. It was surreal and very exciting'.

Meeting the Prince for the first time on the plane and talking to him about the trip and his own illustrative documentary style, Ward soon realised he would be suitable for what the Prince wanted: an artist who could record all aspects of the tour, not through formal drawings and watercolours of places and things, but on an intimate scale in small sketchbooks, like a diary of everything that happened around the Prince, officially and behind the scenes. He reduced his working load to an ink pen, soft pencil and notebook, leaving other drawing and watercolour materials in the car or plane, so he could travel lighter. By the end of the tour, which lasted from 6 to 13 November, the artist had filled two A6 sketchbooks with over 150 pages of images. The pictures, most in pencil with watercolour washes added later, provide a unique insight to a royal tour. Nothing was missed as the artist shadowed the Prince and his entourage throughout. He recorded the numerous briefing sessions, flights, motorcades, arrivals, greetings, speeches, receptions, banquets, private meetings and media scrambles, noting on the page where and when.

All members of the Prince's party feature in the sketches – *Inspector Andy Crichton changes his socks; Elspeth and Mary Anne preparing the Prince's speech, 1.30 am Monday morning; Commander Robert Fraser (Equerry) and Stephen Lamport (Deputy Private Secretary) discuss the next phase of the day.* There is also a record of Jonathan Dimbleby and Philip Bonham Carter working on the documentary *Charles: The Private Man, The Public Role;* of General Sir Peter de la Billière serving as the Prince's personal adviser for the trip; of the accompanying British correspondents and photographers; and of the ubiquitous part of every tour programme involving the British Council, British Embassy, *HMY Britannia*, British businesses and the British community. 'The Prince was always working and meeting people and I was always sketching and drawing. You'd go into these huge banquets and come out far hungrier than when you went in! Fortunately the Prince's personal team were roughly my age and all very relaxed, so it was easy going, but phenomenally busy at the same time'.

Apart from recording the day to day work on tour, Toby Ward's Gulf sketchbooks relate his personal feelings and experiences. After the tour, he wrote to the Prince: 'I had never been to the Gulf before and I was fascinated by what I found, it was completely different from anywhere I had ever seen before. The flatness of the desert in Saudi Arabia and Kuwait was extraordinary and when I made an odd sketch I kept putting the horizon too high on the paper. In Europe our eye is not confronted with such a landscape'.[6] Alongside a couple of quick pencil and wash sketches of the Empty Quarter, he writes of his wonder: 'The silence is the first thing I notice followed by the intense colours of the sand dunes. In each direction there is a different effect of light and

colour to be seen'.[7] This is followed in the sketchbook by a startling double page composition of the Prince being interviewed, with purple shadows cast across the sand dunes in the late afternoon light. The next double page spread shows camels in the desert and notes the striking colour combination of blue, grey, terracotta, red, purple and violet during the magical transformation of the landscape as dusk approaches.

Two watercolour sketches of a visit to ruined houses destroyed during the Gulf War in Kuwait provide a stark contrast to scenes of lavish meals and richly decorated palaces, and dramatically puncture the sketchbook with a powerful reminder of man's inhumanity to man (Cat. 83). The visit to the sandstone cliffs and ruins of the ancient city of Petra in Jordan was another memorable experience for the artist. Arriving on horseback and free to wander and sketch, he was provided with a noteworthy climax to the week away with the Prince (Cat. 87). 'I was absolutely thrilled to go to Petra', Ward wrote to the Prince. 'Years ago I spent many hours copying David Roberts' lithographs of the place, but I never thought I would ever go myself. I scribbled madly during our visit and am now trying to decipher the sketches I made then'.[8]

Toby Ward acknowledges the importance of the Gulf trip to his work: 'It helped set me off on a particular style of working. Soon after I got back, the *Financial Times* asked to use some of the drawings to illustrate an article. The National Trust picked up on this and asked me to do some work for them. My career was finding its direction and the Prince gave me that crucial first opportunity – and I was still only a student'.

9A Lurline Gardens
Battersea
LONDON SW11 4DE

1st December 1993

Sir,

There is no way in which I can thank you enough for inviting me to join your trip to the Gulf. It was a great honour for me and I enjoyed myself immensely from beginning to end.

When Stephen Lamport telephoned me on the Friday before departure, I was just getting ready to go and watch the firework display in Battersea Park. As I watched the display I tried to picture what the trip would be like. I was very excited at the prospect as I made my hasty preparations. I had to pinch myself to ensure I wasn't dreaming as we arrived in Riyadh. (I had originally anticipated spending the evening at the Cinema in Fulham)

I had never been to the Gulf States before and I was fascinated by what I found. It was completely different from anywhere I had ever seen before. The flatness of the desert in Saudi Arabia and Kuwait was extraordinary. When I made the odd sketch I kept putting the horizon too high on the paper. In Europe our eye is not confronted with such a landscape.

I was interested to meet so many people from the countries we visited and I was constantly struck by the strong sense of humour they all seemed to have that often surfaced during the grand banquets. These occasions were marvellous and I did manage to get some of them down in a sketchbook. The mass of people in such splendid settings was a delight to draw. I found the food set out for these banquets amazing. The tables really did groan under the weight of the food.

I was thrilled to stay on board Her Majesty's Yacht Britannia. She is so peaceful and elegant and has a fascinating history, parts of which I learned from the Captain as he gave us a guided tour one evening. I was very impressed by the engine room, for me it is a most beautiful piece of 20th Century sculpture as well as being a fine piece of engineering. It would be a wonderful subject for a careful drawing.

Our trip to the empty quarter has left me with a very strong desire to return there to paint for a longer time. Some years ago I read Wilfred Thesiger's books about the desert but my imagination never prepared me for the brilliance and colour of the place. I sketched as much as I could and made some colour notes from which I am now working. The people there are also wonderful subjects and their camels are such extraordinary creatures that they defy all but the most carefully observed drawing.

It may seem strange but I do enjoy drawing in a busy place as well as in the peaceful countryside. I find working alongside busy people exciting. During the visit to the Dubai Airshow I did not expect to get any drawing done, but when I got down to it I was pleasantly surprised at what could be distilled from such chaotic scenes.

My aim was to record the visit at the pace at which events took place. This was not always successful but it was fun to take on such a challenge.

During our stay in Jordan I was absolutely thrilled to go to Petra. Years ago I spent many hours copying David Robert's lithographs of the place, but I never thought that I would ever go there myself. I scribbled madly during our visit and I am now trying to decypher the sketches I made then.

I certainly never thought that I would enter the city on horseback!

I am slowly working on the sketchbooks and when I have finished them I would like to send them to you to look at. Then I shall try to make some small paintings using the sketches and my memory.

I was so very pleased that you showed me your watercolours which are not only very good but also very professional. To take on landscape painting in so difficult a medium as watercolour is very difficult and to complete them as you do using only watercolour in its purist form is a considerable achievement. I have yet to get to grips with watercolour properly. I tend to cheat by drawing everything out with a pencil first and then filling in the lines with watercolour – my method is not strictly painting!

I was very glad to see the painting you had done in the Alps. I love Alpine country and could happily paint there for a long time. Earlier this year I spent a week in the French Alps, the paintings were quite successful but difficult as my watercolours froze and the cold made my oil paint go curiously lumpy. I do hope that you get many more opportunities to continue your painting.

(something to sit on is essential)

At all times during the visit your whole team was very helpful in every way. They were always so kind and went out of their way to make me feel part of things. I always knew where I was supposed to be going and what I was supposed to be doing as I was so excellently looked after.

Finally I would like to thank you for your Birthday present. It was so very kind and thoughtful of you and it made my twenty eighth birthday one I will never forget. I use the wallet constantly and it will most certainly remind me of the wonderful week I spent with you and your team in the Gulf.

I am your obedient Servant,

Toby Ward

Cat. 88 *Illustrated Letter to HRH The Prince of Wales* 1993

Emma Sergeant

Emma Sergeant was born in 1959 and was first taught drawing by her artist mother, who also encouraged her, while she was at Camden School for Girls, to attend drawing classes two afternoons a week run in Kentish Town by the Inner London Education Authority. She studied in 1978-79 at Camberwell School of Art under Sargy Mann and in 1979-83 at the Slade School of Art. As a student, she won the 1981 National Portrait Gallery Award with an ambitious and complex group composition *Drinks at Milapote.* She was commissioned shortly afterwards by the Gallery to paint portraits of the scholar and writer Lord David Cecil and of the actor Lord Olivier. She was given her first solo exhibition at Agnew's in 1984 and two years later produced a series of paintings of scenes in Afghanistan in aid of UNICEF. Other shows have included *Faces from Four Continents* (1988), which featured portraits and landscapes from around the world; *Orpheus and the Underworld* (1994), a reinterpretation of the Greek myth; and *Gods* (1996), a series of modern portraits of Sumerian gods of the earliest known civilisation, which existed between the Tigris and Euphrates rivers over 5,000 years ago.

Cat. 89 *Head Study, Egypt* 1995

Emma Sergeant has painted numerous commissioned portraits, including the former Foreign Secretary Lord Carrington for the University of Reading; the Nobel prize winner for chemistry Lord Todd, for the Order of Merit series in the Royal Collection; and the inventor of the hovercraft Sir Christopher Cockerell for the National Portrait Gallery. In 1994, HRH The Duke of York commissioned her to paint his portrait. Her most recent exhibition, on the theme of the physical and spiritual beauty of dolphins, was held at the Fine Art Society in June 1998. She lives and has her studio in central London.

HRH The Prince of Wales has followed Emma Sergeant's career since she was a student at the Slade School of Art. He first purchased one of her works in the mid 1980s, *Study for Milapote II*, an oil study for her winning painting for the 1981 National Portrait Gallery Award. She did not meet the Prince, however, until 1994 at an exhibition at Sotheby's of the Prince's watercolours, organised as part of a nationwide tour to mark the 25th anniversary of his investiture as Prince of Wales. Emma Sergeant remembers

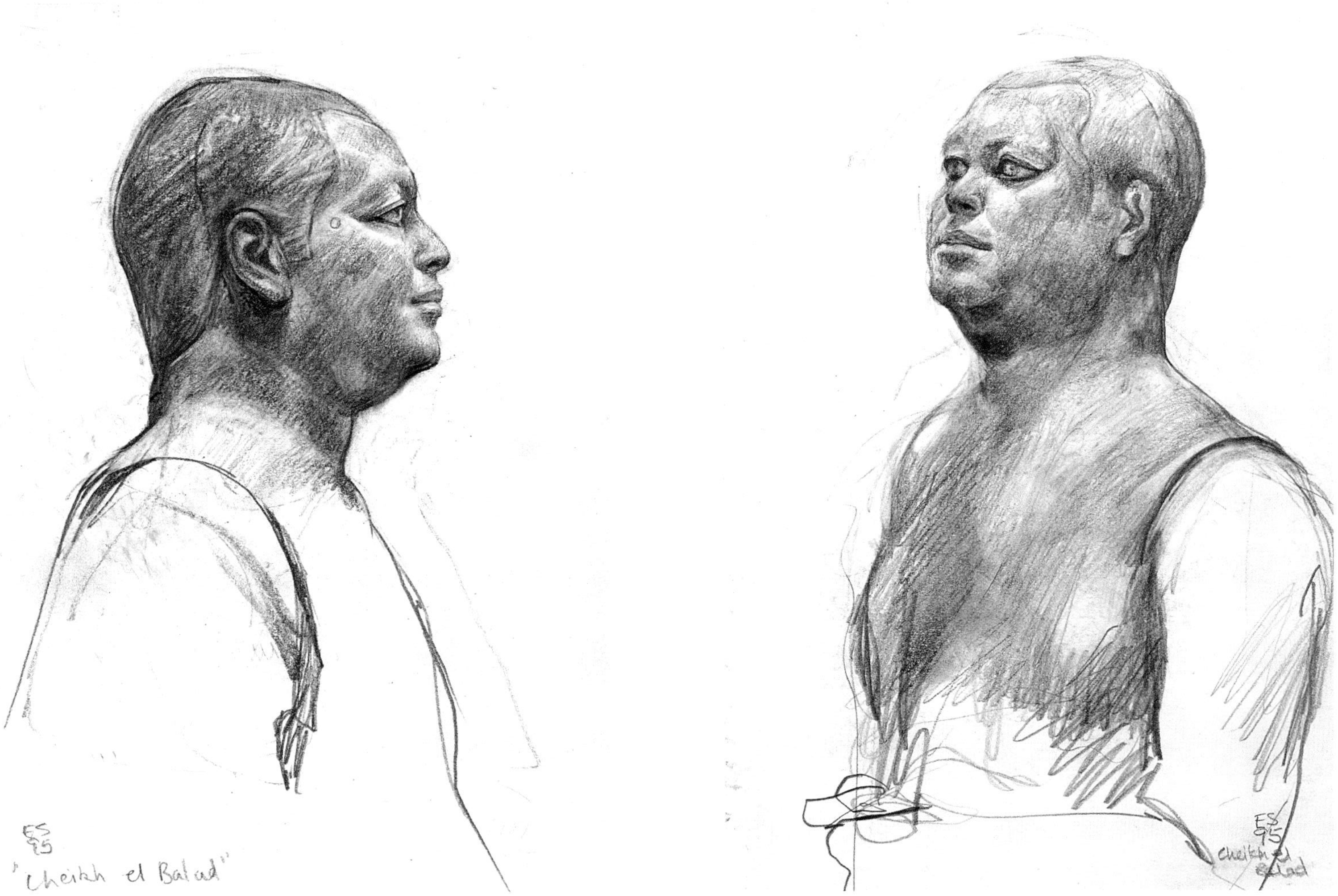

Cat. 90 *Two Head Studies, Egypt* 1995

Opposite: Cat. 91
HRH The Prince of Wales
1995

the occasion: 'I had my nose stuck in the catalogue and was miles away. The next thing, he bounces up to me and says, "I'm your biggest fan". It was so sweet. He said, "I want you to come on a trip I've got coming up which I think will be suitable for you – Morocco and Egypt". I couldn't believe it. This was my dream pilgrimage come true in the most dreamy way. I had longed to go to Egypt'.

The tour party arrived in Cairo late on Saturday 11 March 1995 for three full days in Egypt followed by two days in Morocco. Emma Sergeant found it difficult to fit in to the atmosphere and momentum of the tour, opting to spend much of Sunday and Monday in the Cairo Museum, 'partly from nerves and partly from fascination'. She already knew the most famous exhibits, especially the Tutankhamen treasures, from reproductions, but seeing them and having the time to study them in detail and to sketch was intensely satisfying: 'When I look at all those Egyptian pictures, or tombs, or sphinxes or statues, it strikes a chord which is so deep in me. It's almost like information which has been lying there waiting to be excavated'. She sketched rapidly with a thick lead pencil, producing small but energetic studies. These included two drawings of Sheykh el-Balad (Cat. 90), which the artist considers one of the most significant statues in the museum: 'It's the local tax collector and was carved out of an ancient piece of cedar wood. It has lasted thousands of years. It is so human. It was found by a few local Egyptians, who when it was first dug out of a cave ran out screaming because they thought it was alive!' Sergeant was surprised that the sculpture was bypassed during the Prince's official tour of the museum on the third day of the visit, but was pleased that she had captured something of its unique quality for the Prince in her two drawings of it.

There were many unforgettable moments in Egypt such as the visits to the Coptic Cathedral of Abbassiya and to the 6th century Monastery of St Catherine on Mount Sinai, near the legendary site of the Burning Bush. Nevertheless, the outstanding experience for the artist was a late night trip to Giza on Monday 13 March: 'Walking around the Pyramids and the Sphinx at night is just breathtaking. It was just awesome being there. I've read a lot more about them since. You realise just how amazing the Pyramids must have looked with their white limestone finish and gold tips on the top'. The following day, after the Prince's visit to the Cairo Museum, the tour team flew to Luxor, took the Presidential ferry across the Nile and was driven to the Valley of the Kings to see the tombs of Tutankhamen and Seti I. From there they went to the Temple of Hatshepsut and on to the Valley of the Queens, where they entered Queen Nefertari's tomb and where Emma Sergeant was astonished by the strength of colour of the wall paintings. After crossing to the other side of the Nile, they were driven to Karnak to see the magnificent temple complex of the state god Amon-Re.

Seeing such wonders made a huge impression on the artist. The disciplined process of acute observation and drawing over many years has helped Emma Sergeant to memorise images and store them in her imagination to tap into later in the studio. She found on tour that, during periods of waiting around in reception areas for the Prince's engagements to finish, the excitement of what she was seeing and discovering triggered off bursts of drawing from her imagination. A fine example of this is the *Head Study, Egypt* (Cat. 89), drawn in the foyer of the British Embassy in Cairo: 'It's almost a liberation to work from your memory because if you're always copying, you are sometimes inhibited and instead of feeling the spirit of the place or object, let the whole thing just whistle

Cat. 92 *Three Male Figure Studies, Central Asia* 1996

through you. You can get stuck with very short parameters in having to get absolutely right what you are seeing in front of you'.

Sergeant's impressive set of paintings of Sumerian gods produced after the Egypt trip owe a great deal to her Egyptian experience, especially in the pose, stillness and sculptural presence of the figures. The Prince of Wales visited the *Gods* exhibition at Agnew's and was shown around by the artist. He was fascinated by her bold reinterpretation of such a subject for a contemporary audience. Later, during a visit to her studio in summer 1997, he was able to see some of the paintings again, and acquired his favourite from the series, *Ninib*, the god of Saturn and deity of hunters and strength (Fig. 12). This impressive painting now hangs in pride of place in the new Orchard Room at Highgrove.

The visit to Morocco from 15 to 18 March 1995 provided an extraordinary contrast to Emma Sergeant's previous visit as 'a tourist in jeans'. The first day of engagements on Thursday started with a crammed morning in Fez, the oldest of Morocco's four imperial cities and a centre for traditional crafts, trade and learning. These included a tour around the Qarawiyin Mosque, the oldest mosque in North Africa, and a walk around the R'Cif market (the artist later sketched the Prince in a Fez hat). On occasions she failed to keep up with the group: 'You look the wrong way for a minute and everybody's gone! I was busy sketching in an Islamic school and after a while thought that everything had gone a bit quiet. No one had bothered to fetch me. I went out into a little market outside and asked people which way for the royal party? Prince? Which way? Luckily they all agreed on which direction. So I ran and ran and ran. I finally caught up with the back of a crowd. You're over the first hurdle as you've found them. The second hurdle is to get from the back end of the crowd to the security people,

Cat. 93 *Three Female Studies, Central Asia* 1996

who don't know who you are, to the security people at the front, who do, and then back inside the royal group'. The following and final day of the tour, while the Prince went to Casablanca on official engagements, Emma Sergeant travelled to Marrakesh to shop and sketch in the market. She arrived back in London the next day physically and mentally exhausted but brimming with ideas.

Emma Sergeant was a natural choice for the Prince's tour to the Ukraine and the Central Asian Republics of Turkmenistan, Kazakhstan, Kyrgyzstan and Uzbekistan, which took place from 4 to 12 November 1996. Her work revealed a fascination with the human face and its endless variations around the world. Here was an opportunity to study the features of different peoples – Tartar, Turkmen, Kazakh, Kyrgyz and Uzbek – and their cultural traditions, across a vast area of Central Asia, which had been hidden from the West for decades. Like the Prince, she was also interested in gaining a wider understanding of the varying traditions of Islam, to see the stunning mosques and to experience the flat sunbaked landscapes, fertile oases and foothills of mountain ranges.

Emma Sergeant learned a great deal from Keith Critchlow, an expert on Islamic visual arts who accompanied the tour: she found out how to look at the architecture; how it was built and used by the people; how to identify regional styles; and what could be done to conserve what had survived the Soviet era. She was uncertain at the start of the tour whether to draw the buildings or the people, deciding eventually on the latter: 'The trouble with drawing the architecture was that it was so extraordinarily beautiful you began to wonder what was the point of dashing off something anecdotal which couldn't possibly capture the magnificence of it all'. One of her first drawings of the tour was a forceful head study of the robust features of Leonid Kuchma, the President of the Ukraine, done during a visit by the Prince to the Mariyinsky Palace in Kiev for an official dinner. The next day the party flew to Crimea to tour Bakhchisaray to see the historical Tartar Khan's Palace and visit a Crimean Tartar family, followed by a tour of the Balaklava battlefield and a visit to Sevastopol. The artist was looking forward to sketching some Crimean Tartars, a people exiled after the Second World War to Central Asia and Siberia and, though legally rehabilitated in the 1960s, prevented from returning to their homeland; but she was saddened to find no opportunity.

The following day, Emma Sergeant left Yalta in the Crimea and flew with the tour group to Ashkhabad, the capital of Turkmenistan, which lies in a spectacular natural setting of an oasis at the foot of a mountain range and at the edge of a desert. The two day visit was filled with official functions, including the opening of the British Embassy, and ended with a visual treat: a tour of Merv, the ancient Islamic city in the Mary region. By the time she had arrived in Kazakhstan much of Sergeant's drawing focused on portraits of ordinary people, most in their region's style of dress, some of whom posed for a few minutes. These included a woman behind the ticket counter at the Central State Museum; another who passed by in the street and was drawn from memory; and a student at the Kazakh State Academy of Architecture and Construction who was dancing in her national costume outside during the Prince's visit to inaugurate a course on environmental management (Cat. 93).

The day visit to Kyrgyzstan typified the range of subjects available to the artist: a meeting with the Mayor in the City Hall; visits to a home for the elderly and a new born and premature babies hospital; a meeting with President Akayev; a demonstration of Kyrgyz dancing, music and sports; lunch in a nomad's tent; a tree planting; a walk through a market; and finally a reception hosted by the British Ambassador. This last was enlivened by a recital by one of the country's finest singers, whom Sergeant sketched to add to her portrait gallery of the tour, before the dash to the airport and a flight to Tashkent in Uzbekistan.

For Emma Sergeant the final Uzbek stretch of the visit to Central Asia, to see the archaeological and architectural splendours of the ancient cities of Samarkand and Bukhara, was a fitting climax to her extraordinary artistic journey through Islam with the Prince. Nevertheless, it was not the Samarkand Gur-e Amir mausoleum for the 14th century Mongol conqueror Timur, crowned with its beautiful dome and walled with turquoise arabesques and gold inscriptions which she drew; nor the picturesque sweep of mosques, bazaars and flat roofed, sun-dried brick houses of the old town in Bukhara: 'Both the Prince and I were moved by the dignity of the people as we walked around. We went to a tea house in Bukhara with lots of old men in their traditional coats sitting around. The Prince said to me as I was sketching, "Don't miss the one in purple", so I stayed and did a quick drawing in about five minutes. Poor Commander Lavery, the Prince's Equerry, had to stand with me while I worked away. The cars were revving their engines outside ready to go to the airport to take us back to Tashkent! I really should have been drawing there all day' (Cat. 92).

Reviewing her two tours with the Prince, Emma Sergeant concludes: 'They were both trips at moments when I really needed the support. The great lesson to me about travelling with his group of people was that everybody is very conscious of the fact that they are ambassadors. You're with them and the rest of the world slides by like a strange film show. That is the unreality. Your reality is all these people scrabbling around who each day are trying to keep the show on the road, immaculately. And, of course, you're under as much pressure as they are. You can all fall apart with hysterics like children in private moments out of the public gaze'.

Cat. 93 *Three Female Studies, Central Asia* 1996

who don't know who you are, to the security people at the front, who do, and then back inside the royal group'. The following and final day of the tour, while the Prince went to Casablanca on official engagements, Emma Sergeant travelled to Marrakesh to shop and sketch in the market. She arrived back in London the next day physically and mentally exhausted but brimming with ideas.

Emma Sergeant was a natural choice for the Prince's tour to the Ukraine and the Central Asian Republics of Turkmenistan, Kazakhstan, Kyrgyzstan and Uzbekistan, which took place from 4 to 12 November 1996. Her work revealed a fascination with the human face and its endless variations around the world. Here was an opportunity to study the features of different peoples – Tartar, Turkmen, Kazakh, Kyrgyz and Uzbek – and their cultural traditions, across a vast area of Central Asia, which had been hidden from the West for decades. Like the Prince, she was also interested in gaining a wider understanding of the varying traditions of Islam, to see the stunning mosques and to experience the flat sunbaked landscapes, fertile oases and foothills of mountain ranges.

Emma Sergeant learned a great deal from Keith Critchlow, an expert on Islamic visual arts who accompanied the tour: she found out how to look at the architecture; how it was built and used by the people; how to identify regional styles; and what could be done to conserve what had survived the Soviet era. She was uncertain at the start of the tour whether to draw the buildings or the people, deciding eventually on the latter: 'The trouble with drawing the architecture was that it was so extraordinarily beautiful you began to wonder what was the point of dashing off something anecdotal which couldn't possibly capture the magnificence of it all'. One of her first drawings of the tour was a forceful head study of the robust features of Leonid Kuchma, the President of the Ukraine, done during a visit by the Prince to the Mariyinsky Palace in Kiev for an official dinner. The next day the party flew to Crimea to tour Bakhchisaray to see the historical Tartar Khan's Palace and visit a Crimean Tartar family, followed by a tour of the Balaklava battlefield and a visit to Sevastopol. The artist was looking forward to sketching some Crimean Tartars, a people exiled after the Second World War to Central Asia and Siberia and, though legally rehabilitated in the 1960s, prevented from returning to their homeland; but she was saddened to find no opportunity.

The following day, Emma Sergeant left Yalta in the Crimea and flew with the tour group to Ashkhabad, the capital of Turkmenistan, which lies in a spectacular natural setting of an oasis at the foot of a mountain range and at the edge of a desert. The two day visit was filled with official functions, including the opening of the British Embassy, and ended with a visual treat: a tour of Merv, the ancient Islamic city in the Mary region. By the time she had arrived in Kazakhstan much of Sergeant's drawing focused on portraits of ordinary people, most in their region's style of dress, some of whom posed for a few minutes. These included a woman behind the ticket counter at the Central State Museum; another who passed by in the street and was drawn from memory; and a student at the Kazakh State Academy of Architecture and Construction who was dancing in her national costume outside during the Prince's visit to inaugurate a course on environmental management (Cat. 93).

The day visit to Kyrgyzstan typified the range of subjects available to the artist: a meeting with the Mayor in the City Hall; visits to a home for the elderly and a new born and premature babies hospital; a meeting with President Akayev; a demonstration of Kyrgyz dancing, music and sports; lunch in a nomad's tent; a tree planting; a walk through a market; and finally a reception hosted by the British Ambassador. This last was enlivened by a recital by one of the country's finest singers, whom Sergeant sketched to add to her portrait gallery of the tour, before the dash to the airport and a flight to Tashkent in Uzbekistan.

For Emma Sergeant the final Uzbek stretch of the visit to Central Asia, to see the archaeological and architectural splendours of the ancient cities of Samarkand and Bukhara, was a fitting climax to her extraordinary artistic journey through Islam with the Prince. Nevertheless, it was not the Samarkand Gur-e Amir mausoleum for the 14th century Mongol conqueror Timur, crowned with its beautiful dome and walled with turquoise arabesques and gold inscriptions which she drew; nor the picturesque sweep of mosques, bazaars and flat roofed, sun-dried brick houses of the old town in Bukhara: 'Both the Prince and I were moved by the dignity of the people as we walked around. We went to a tea house in Bukhara with lots of old men in their traditional coats sitting around. The Prince said to me as I was sketching, "Don't miss the one in purple", so I stayed and did a quick drawing in about five minutes. Poor Commander Lavery, the Prince's Equerry, had to stand with me while I worked away. The cars were revving their engines outside ready to go to the airport to take us back to Tashkent! I really should have been drawing there all day' (Cat. 92).

Reviewing her two tours with the Prince, Emma Sergeant concludes: 'They were both trips at moments when I really needed the support. The great lesson to me about travelling with his group of people was that everybody is very conscious of the fact that they are ambassadors. You're with them and the rest of the world slides by like a strange film show. That is the unreality. Your reality is all these people scrabbling around who each day are trying to keep the show on the road, immaculately. And, of course, you're under as much pressure as they are. You can all fall apart with hysterics like children in private moments out of the public gaze'.

Susannah Fiennes

Susannah Fiennes was born in 1961 and studied under Euan Uglow at the Slade School of Art in 1979-83, where she graduated with a first class degree. She was included in the *Pick of Graduate Art* exhibition at Christie's in 1983 and in the *Young Contemporaries* show at Agnew's in 1988. In 1991, she was artist-in-residence at Hambros Bank, New York. She has exhibited at the Cadogan Contemporary gallery and at the National Portrait Gallery BP Award, from which she won the BP Travel Award in 1993. Inspired by Jung Chang's *Wild Swans*, she used the award to fund a two-month painting expedition across China in 1994. Before leaving, she met Jung Chang and painted her mother, Mrs Xia De-hong. On her return, she had an exhibition, *Chinese Characters,* at the National Portrait Gallery. She has had solo exhibitions at the Grundy Art Gallery, Blackpool, of her paintings of Blackpool beach, and at the Wigmore Hall. In summer 1995, she was artist-in-residence at the Khumo Chamber Music Festival, Finland. Susannah Fiennes has also taught art at Dulwich College in 1985-87, and run a private art class in Westminster 1987-93 and teaches painting courses for Westminster Classic Tours in Turkey. Her most recent exhibition of paintings relating to her trip to China, and of the Hong Kong handover of 1997 was held at the Rafael Valls Gallery in London in summer 1998. She lives in Kennington and has her studio in Clapham, South London.

Cat. 96 *HRH The Prince of Wales Painting in Oman* 1995

Susannah Fiennes was recommended to HRH The Prince of Wales by Emma Sergeant, a fellow student at the Slade School of Art. Fiennes's work abroad, her ability to draw quickly and to fit in with a team (evident from her artist residencies), all made her an ideal candidate for the Oman tour, which took place from 1 to 6 October 1995. The artist was briefed at St James's Palace a week before the trip about the dress code of a Muslim country.

As with all the Prince's tours, there was little time to adjust to the country before the tour programme was in full swing: 'Working in that heat and humidity was extremely difficult. I was exhausted from the jetlag, but was determined to work hard and the adrenalin kept me going'. On the first morning, she joined the the artist Sue Phipps, a friend of the Prince who was living in Oman, for a morning working in Muscat market, while the Prince attended meetings at the Bait al Barakah Palace and the Ministry of Justice, and attended a lunch with Omani businessmen. The market was teeming with activity and Fiennes found it hard to decide what to draw first, but knew that in the limited time she wanted to do as much as possible: 'I sat and drew one figure and I was soon surrounded by men of all ages. They became my models for the next two hours. It felt like a performance in front of an audience. At this stage I had no idea how I would use these drawings when I got home. I'd never really worked like this before. I came back from the tour with four drawing books filled'.

In the afternoon Susannah Fiennes rejoined the tour party for a Red Arrows flying display at Seeb Airport attended by Omani VIPs and 200 members of the British community. The event provided her with a key motif for the paintings she was later to produce in London: the standing, robed Arab figure like a column of colour shimmering in the heat: 'From then, I noticed these wonderful figures standing. They were a recurring theme. The whites and purples of their robes were beautiful against their dark warm skin' (Cat. 95).

The next day the Prince and his party flew to Salalah in the south of Oman for a day of engagements with Sultan Qaboos bin Said. While the Prince had a private audience with the Sultan at the al Hosn palace and various other meetings, Susannah drew the Sultan's staff who, intrigued, queued up in the Sultan's palace to pose for her. Even the Minister for Water Resources and the Minister of Culture sat for the artist, while they waited for their meetings to take place. The day ended with an evening of lively dancing and music.

As guests of the Prince's friends, Sue and Jeremy Phipps, the final two days were private and therefore more relaxed. Susannah Fiennes recalls: 'The Prince and a few of us flew into the desert in a Hercules, which was thrilling, and then by helicopter for some short hops. The Prince was taken on a long walk, so I tried to do some painting. The water evaporated so quickly I couldn't do anything and with no shade, it was too hot to paint'.

The party was then taken to see the endangered Arabian oryx, reintroduced into the wild by the Sultan. On the way they met two Bedouin tribesmen sitting under a fig tree, which provided the only shade for miles around. The Bedou asked the Prince and his small party to sit with them on a rug and gave them figs and coffee. Susannah Fiennes sat down and drew them both. It was a compelling moment for her: 'I drew them with their heads bowed and felt there was something moving about them. Later, back in my studio, I developed this idea in a watercolour (Cat. 94) and oil painting. Looking through my Oman portfolio, the Prince immediately chose these pictures which suggests he was also touched by that moment'.

The Prince and his artist had an opportunity to paint with each other in the late afternoon in the desert. She chose to paint the Prince doing a watercolour of the landscape as the sun was setting:

Cat. 94 *Turbanned Head* 1995

Cat. 95 *Four Standing Figures, Oman* 1995

'He was wearing a beautiful yellow shirt, creamy stone coloured trousers with rust coloured desert boots, which was all so harmonious with the desert' (Cat. 96). On the final day, the artist flew in a helicopter with the Prince to the Jebal Akhdar mountains in the north. While the Prince again went on a long walk in the morning, she painted the landscape, but found it too overwhelming a subject to express in a few quick watercolours. In the late afternoon, the Prince painted with her for a couple of hours. She turned to paint him again, not least because he provided a useful focal point in the landscape: 'He also happened to be wearing a combination of green and grey which looked beautiful against the rusty stone and the purple distant hills; a perfect harmony of secondary colours'.

After the painting session Jeremy Phipps appeared amused and puzzled by her painting: 'The Prince generously defended me and said "Jeremy, you have to understand the whole Slade approach. It's not to do with imitating the subject, but with seeing it as an arrangement of abstract shapes". I was impressed by the Prince's understanding'.

On the flight back to London a few hours later, the Prince and Susannah Fiennes compared notes and had a brief critique of each

Cat. 97 *HMY Britannia in Hong Kong Harbour* 1997

other's painting: 'We had had this beautiful day in the mountains and were suddenly being transported back to reality. Arriving at 8 o'clock on Friday morning at St James's Palace, everybody goes their separate ways. It's very much business as usual'.

Two years later, in 1997, Susannah Fiennes was back with the Prince and his team on a tour to Hong Kong from 27 June to 4 July, to include the British farewell and handover ceremonies on 30 June. She had been telephoned by Stephen Lamport the previous March to see if she was free to go, but was asked to keep the matter secret for six weeks. She knew that this would be a far bigger trip than Oman, as the world's eyes would be on Hong Kong for such an historical and politically sensitive moment. In Oman, she had mostly recorded the people. 'Do anything you like', the Prince said on the plane to Hong Kong. It was clear to her that a key symbolic image would be the Royal Yacht in Hong Kong Harbour. Not only was it the end of a British Crown Colony but it was also the last official voyage of *HMY Britannia.*

As usual, *HMY Britannia* was their base for the trip and was to be used for official receptions and dinners. Susannah went straight out for the afternoon to paint watercolour views of the yacht and the harbour, against a backdrop of skyscrapers. She established a routine of fitting in two to three hour painting sessions in between the functions she needed to attend, leaving enough time to change for an official luncheon, drinks reception or black tie dinner. The role of artist extended to that of house guest.

The next day she attended a church service on *HMY Britannia*, the last while the yacht was on official duty. Although she had been on the Royal Yacht for less than 24 hours, it was an emotional moment for her as it offered all those present, including the Prince, a half hour for quiet reflection and prayer away from the busy schedule. Later, accompanied by two officers (who carried her paints), she took the ferry to Kowloon on the mainland to paint the Hong Kong skyline. Then she painted two views of *HMY Britannia* from the Tamar reclamation site (Cat. 97), where the farewell ceremony would be taking place the next day. It was an intimidating experience as the area was designated high security and there were guards everywhere. In the evening, the Prince gave a formal dinner on *HMY Britannia* attended by Chris Patten, the last Governor of Hong Kong, and by many British politicians, including past Prime Ministers.

On the day of the handover, with such tight security and wet weather, Susannah Fiennes was unable to go far from the Royal Yacht. Tony Blair, the Prime Minister, and Mrs Blair visited the Prince during the afternoon, but it was not possible to draw at the Prince's private meetings on board. She recalls: 'There was a wonderful moment as everyone gathered, including the Pattens, ready to leave for the handover ceremony. The Prince wore a dashing uniform. It was like being backstage at some incredible opera when the lead singer is about to go out and perform. At the ceremony, I got a good vantage point from the top of a stand, but couldn't see a thing because of the umbrellas and couldn't hear because of the rain on the metal stand. It was disappointing, but back in my studio in London, I started to work on paintings from memory. The yellow and blue umbrellas were a wonderful decorative subject and the mood was highly charged'.

The schedule for the rest of the evening was intensely busy – a firework display in the harbour; an official banquet for over 3,000 guests in the New Convention Centre hosted by Robin Cook, the Foreign Secretary; and the handover ceremony which took place at midnight. Susannah Fiennes had only a brief opportunity to draw in the ante room before the ceremony began: 'I drew the Prince and Tony Blair, who were sitting together talking informally. Stupidly, I had forgotten my glasses, so my drawings of them are rather vague'.

After the ceremony, Susannah Fiennes boarded *HMY Britannia* with the rest of the party, including Chris Patten and his family: 'Leaving the harbour in the early hours of the morning was extraordinary. I'll never forget that sensation of parting as the yacht moved away from the quay'.

During the two day sea voyage to Manila in the Philippines, where the Prince had half a day of engagements on 3 July before the party flew back to London, the artist saw Chris Patten on deck leaning on the railing, looking back. It was a potent image which later, back in her studio, she explored in a group of watercolours (Cat. 98) and oils. It seemed to her a metaphor for the farewells and parting: a valedictory moment in history. The Prince added an oil painting and a watercolour of the scene to his collection. The artist later gave a portrait drawing of Patten, made on the Royal Yacht, to the National Portrait Gallery.

Cat. 98 *Christopher Patten Leaving Hong Kong* 1997

Robert Wraith

Robert Wraith was born in 1952, and educated at Stowe, which he left at 16. He was invited by Pietro Annigoni to study with him in Florence, instead of going to art school, and later worked as his assistant on various frescoes in churches, learning the techniques of the Italian Renaissance masters. In the mid 1970s, he moved back to England permanently and established himself as a painter of portraits, genre scenes and landscapes. He has had 14 one man shows, including one at the Christ Church Picture Gallery, Oxford, in 1985, and has been represented by leading London galleries, including the Belgrave Gallery, Berkeley Square Gallery, St James's Art Group and John Martin. His pictures are regularly shown at the Royal Academy Summer Exhibition, the Royal Society of Portrait Painters and the Royal Watercolour Society. A prize winner of the *Hunting Group* exhibition in 1984, he was chosen by the art critic Brian Sewell for the *Discerning Eye* exhibition in 1990. His portrait commissions have included the Archbishop of Canterbury, Robert Runcie, in 1982. An allegorical painting by the artist on the theme of Thomas à Becket was presented by the Archbishop to Pope John Paul II during the Papal visit of 1982. He has recently painted a half length portrait of HM The Queen, commissioned by Shell UK to mark its 100th anniversary, which was produced during sittings at Buckingham Palace and unveiled in May 1998. Robert Wraith's work is held in the collections of Oxford University, Eton College, the Vatican, the MCC, the Royal College of General Practitioners and the National Trust. He lives and has his studio in Oxfordshire.

Cat. 100 *Coronation of King Letsie III, Lesotho: Figure on Horse* 1997

HRH The Prince of Wales looked through a portfolio of work by Robert Wraith on the recommendation of John Ward and selected him to be the official artist for his tour to Swaziland, Lesotho and South Africa from 28 October to 6 November 1997. The Prince and his party flew out on the evening of Tuesday 28th from London to Johannesburg, where they transferred for a flight to Matsapha airport for the first two days of the tour to Swaziland, a small landlocked country with a monarchy administered by traditional tribal institutions.

The trip comprised a tight schedule of engagements, including meetings at the Parliament Building; a Commonwealth Development Corporation lunch; audiences with King Mswati III at the Lozitha Palace and with The Queen Mother at the Ludzidzini Royal

Kraal; and, on the second day, visits to an industrial site to see a Cadbury's factory, to a water project and to primary schools. The culture of the Bantu-speaking Swazi people featured prominently, most memorably in the reed dancing, music plays and songs accompanied by buck horn whistles, rattles, reed flutes and the rhythmic percussion of shields (Cat. 99). Robert Wraith had never been to Africa before: 'Swaziland was simple and unsophisticated and to experience the timeless tribal life and the stunning landscape was wonderful'.

Although he took oil and watercolour painting boxes and drawing books of different sizes, he realised that at such an electric pace, he could record the experience only through rapid sketches done on a small scale in a drawing book he carried around with him. He had been doing this for years, never using photographs or attempting to reinvent the moment in the studio afterwards by producing larger works from drawings, despite the commercial temptation.

On Thursday evening, the tour moved to the mountainous, diamond-rich independent kingdom of Lesotho, an enclave in the central part of South Africa. The principal event was the coronation of King Letsie III, which took place the following morning in a sports stadium in the capital, Maseru. The spectacle lasted four hours and provided an opportunity for the artist to sit still and draw for more than just a few minutes. He worked extremely fast, covering pages in his drawing book with ink and wash sketches of the horsemen and dancers, their repetitive movement making it easier to record actions and dress (Cat. 100). The climax of the ceremony came when the King put on animal skins and was driven around the stadium to cheering crowds.

An hour later, the Prince and his entourage flew to Pretoria, the capital of the Transvaal and the administrative centre of South Africa, arriving mid afternoon for the start of a six day visit. The city, famous for the jacaranda trees which line the streets, was radiant

Cat. 99 *Studies of Dancing Figure, Ngculwini, Swaziland* 1997

Cat. 102 *The Spice Girls in Concert in Aid of the Nations Trust, Johannesburg* 1997

Below: Cat. 103 *Helicopter to Dukuduku* 1997

with trusses of their vivid blue-purple flowers. The Prince was staying at the Presidential Guest House, where Robert Wraith settled down early next morning to paint a small oil of one of the jacaranda trees in the garden. 'I barely had the colours with me to match the subtlety of the flowers', he admits. The following day, President Nelson Mandela received the Prince at Mahlamba Ndlopfu, his residence. After inspecting a guard of honour and attending a media call, the Prince had an informal lunch with Mandela at which the artist drew them deep in conversation, his drawing book and pencil crayon hidden under the table as he worked (Cat. 101).

The President's secretary, who was sitting beside the artist, enthused about the drawing as she saw it emerge on the paper, but the artist, fearful that the opportunity would be lost if the attention of fellow guests was drawn to him sketching, whispered to her to keep it a secret. The meeting with Mandela, whose dignity and humanity deeply impressed all members of the Prince's party, was one of the highlights of the tour.

After the lunch, the Prince and his group travelled to Johannesburg, rejoining Prince Harry, who had flown out from London with them for a safari holiday with a schoolfriend. After a series of engagements in the afternoon, the Prince and his son attended a Saturday night Spice Girls concert in aid of the Nation's Trust at the Johannesburg Athletics Stadium. Robert Wraith sat with the royal party, sketching in the semi darkness, having to guess the colours. The picture (Cat. 102) shows the brightly lit stage, huge video screen and audience against the spectacular backdrop of the surrounding hills, which flicker with distant lights.

On Sunday, a private day, the Prince took Prince Harry to Fugitive's Drift near Dundee in Natal. They toured the sites of two battles of the Zulu War in 1879: Isandhlwana, where a British force of over 1,500 was annihilated, and Rorke's Drift, where 150 British soldiers defended themselves against 4,000 Zulus and won 11 Victoria Crosses. As Colonel-in-Chief of the Royal Regiment of Wales, whose forerunner, the 24th Regiment of Foot, fought at Rorke's Drift, the Prince later told journalists accompanying the tour that he had gone to pay his respects to the wasted lives on both sides and had found the memorials and the landscape extremely moving. At Isandhlwana, Robert Wraith painted an oil of the scene, showing the stone cairns, which indicated the location of mass burials, and the memorial statue as distant flecks in a broad landscape.

The following day, the artist accompanied the Prince of Wales and Prince Harry in a helicopter to the St Lucia Nature Reserve in KwaZulu, famous for its hundreds of species of birds, as well as crocodiles and hippopotamuses. He later sketched the Princes in the helicopter (Cat. 103) as it took them to North Dukuduku village for a visit to a high school. In the afternoon, the party visited the Kwamakutha township in Durban, toured Durban harbour in a launch and attended civic functions. Wherever they went, Wraith stayed on the edge of things: 'I was able to work more efficiently. You had a captive audience, as the people were all looking at the Prince'.

Tuesday started with a flight from Durban to Cape Town and a visit to the Crossroads township to see a housing and community police project, and ended with a state dinner hosted by President Mandela: from sorrowful deprivation and desperation to almost

Cat. 101 *Mahlamba Ndlopfu, Lunch with President Mandela* 1997

Above: Cat. 104 *Studies of Woman with British Flag, Crossroads, Capetown* 1997

Centre: Cat. 105 *Standing Figure, Crossroads, Capetown* 1997

Right: Cat. 106 *Johannesburg* 1997

unimaginable grandeur. It was typical of the extraordinary contrasts to be experienced on a royal tour. During the two hours the Prince toured Crossroads, Robert Wraith sketched from the back of a minibus, producing some of his finest work on the tour: a steadfast woman in a crowd clutching her Union Jack (Cat. 104); a man standing alongside a ramshackle building, arms folded, his momentary curiosity and his resignation perfectly recorded in a flurry of line and wash (Cat. 105); and a series of lively portrait studies of men in caps.

The final day of the tour included visits in Cape Town to the Kirstenbosch National Botanical Gardens; the South African Museum for a reception given by the British High Commissioner; and the Ravensmead Clinic to view a tuberculosis awareness project; with a Business Leaders Forum seminar at the British Consulate in Johannesburg in the early evening before the flight back to London. Robert Wraith produced over 60 drawings and sketches during the tour. He was left drained by the experience but exhilarated by the countries visited: 'To be given an opportunity to work in that context and experience the visual richness was an amazing gift for which I'm deeply grateful. To go to another continent keeps the eye alive. It didn't change the way I worked. It enriched it'.

James Hart Dyke

James Hart Dyke was born in 1966 and started painting from an early age. He studied architecture at Manchester University in 1986-89 and the Royal College of Art in 1990-92. During the summer of 1992, he decided to make painting his profession. He began by painting visuals for architects. The painter John Ward gave critiques of his work and advised him to copy Old Master paintings at the National Gallery. Hart Dyke's first commission to paint a view of a house came from the interior designer Tessa Kennedy and he has made this genre his speciality. Other commissions have included Pembroke College, Cambridge, and Stonor Park, Oxfordshire, for Lord Camoys. He was included in the National Trust's Centenary exhibition at Christie's in 1995 and in *The Artist and the Country House* exhibition at Sotheby's in 1996.

James Hart Dyke has been a tutor and painter for architectural and planning proposals made by The Prince of Wales's Institute of Architecture Summer Schools: in Viterbo, Italy in 1994 and Biarritz in 1995; and for The Prince of Wales's Urban Design Task Force in Potsdam, Germany, in 1996, and Sidon, Lebanon and Berlin in 1997. He obtained a Higher Diploma in Postgraduate Studies in Painting from the City and Guilds of London Art School, where he studied from 1995-96. While there, he won a national competition for British art schools, to paint a portrait of HRH The Princess Royal for the Royal Society of Osteopaths. In 1996, he was selected for the BP Portrait Award exhibition at the National Portrait Gallery. He lives in London and has his studio in Clerkenwell.

HRH The Prince of Wales first met James Hart Dyke and saw his work at the The Prince of Wales's Institute of Architecture Summer Schools and during his visits to the Urban Design Task Force in the early 1990s. Contacted by the Prince's office at St James's Palace in early January 1998, the artist had only a month to prepare for the 12 day tour, which started on 2 February, to Sri Lanka, Nepal and Bhutan. The Prince's Assistant Private Secretary, Nick Archer, advised about everything from inoculations to black tie. Tropical kit was needed for Sri Lanka and arctic wear for Nepal.

Two hours into the flight from RAF Brize Norton to Colombo, the capital of Sri Lanka, the official tour artist was summoned to the front of the plane: 'I had dinner with the Prince flying somewhere over Italy. I suppose the idea is to try to get the artist to be more relaxed with the situation because you're thrown from one world into another. That morning I was out painting someone's house. And in the evening I was invited to dinner with the Prince of Wales!'

The arrival in Colombo at lunchtime on 3 February was a tense moment for everyone as there was a high level of security because of the Tamil Tiger threat. From the plane window, Hart Dyke could see marksmen in the fields and on the roofs. The arrival ceremony did not quite turn out as planned. The twenty-one gun salute set fire to the grass; the fire engines arrived to hose it down and hosed all the soldiers as well; while in the background he could hear the band playing the theme tune to *Monty Python.*

During the four days in Sri Lanka, most of which were spent in Colombo, he filled his notebook with sketches of places, events and people. These included a Courtauld's clothing factory; the Raja Maha Vihara temple; the botanical gardens; Colombo cricket ground; and dinners at the President's House and at the Queen's House. Hart Dyke sketched the Houses of Parliament, the National Museum and other prominent buildings while the Prince was on official engagements inside. There was no time to work any of these up into an oil sketch: 'Colombo is not a particularly beautiful place, but has a fascinating architectural mixture and I was interested to see how the city worked'. Sketching the parade for the 50th anniversary of Sri Lankan independence, he glimpsed,

Cat. 107 *View towards Himalayas, Nepal* 1998

behind people's heads, one of the most moving images of the tour: 'After the tanks, planes and commando units, it was very touching to see a group of 30 wounded soldiers come past in wheelchairs and on crutches. It struck me as something a country would not normally do. They would try and hide the realities of war. There was a loud cheer for them'.

After visiting a cashew nut processing plant in Gampola on Friday morning, the Prince and his party flew to Kathmandu in Nepal. James Hart Dyke recalls: 'I did some sketches looking out of the window of the plane, flying over India and the Ganges. It was exciting. You sensed you were travelling somewhere very different now. You could see the Himalayan mountains in the distance'.

The next morning the artist flew with the Prince in a helicopter from Kathmandu to Kushma, and drove from there in Land Rovers to Patichaur. A three hour walk took them to the project sites of Nepal-UK Forestry and WaterAid. 'As we walked', Hart Dyke recalls, 'children came rushing down the hills like a waterfall, running across the fields and tumbling down the terraces. It was like a biblical scene. It was difficult to sketch at the time because it was all so fast. But the memories are potent. The joy on the faces of the children when they saw the Prince was fantastic. Hundreds followed him through the valley'.

Cat. 108 *View South of Kathmandu, Nepal* 1998

In the evening they returned to Kathmandu, where there was a reception in the British Ambassador's residence. Hart Dyke met a British artist, Jan Salter, who had lived in the region since the 1960s, and she offered to take him to her favourite painting spots. Early next morning, they set out for the mountains: 'We had breakfast in a small hotel. Outside there was a mist and we couldn't see anything at all. But suddenly it lifted and I saw an amazing panorama of the Himalayas. The light was very sharp and intense and the scale of everything was staggering'. Immediately he started a small oil sketch on panel, which took half an hour (Cat. 107). He intentionally restricted his oil palette for the tour to only five colours – French ultramarine, cadmium yellow, light red, raw umber and white – and had prepared the panels with rabbit skin glue and primer before leaving England. During the day, he painted small oil paintings of the stepped terraces of the mountain side, a view of the valley, and a large temple and ancient square in the town of Bhaktapur. 'It's one of those places where you need to spend a couple of months to get rid of all the obvious paintings you would do and then start something more interesting. I would like to go back to explore other avenues'.

The next day the Prince and his entourage flew from Nepal to Paro in Bhutan. James Hart Dyke sketched Mount Everest as he

Cat. 109 *Paro Dzong, Bhutan* 1998

flew by: 'It is amazing. You're at 24,000 feet and Everest is still rising above you!' The arrival at Paro was a nerve-wracking experience, as the aeroplane dived between the mountains to land on the short runway strip. The Prince and his group were taken to the nearby Kyichu temple, the Ugyen Pelri Palace, to see some archery and dancing, and to the dzong, a massive building which served as a religious, education and administrative centre. Everyone was in national dress. The artist felt as though he had gone back to the medieval age. He was fascinated by the architecture, all of which was traditional: 'The dzong was on a scale I couldn't comprehend. Its windows were 30-40 feet high. It was such an overwhelming subject, I returned to it the next day from the capital Thimphu, where we were staying, and painted two small oil paintings of it. Back in my studio in London, I painted large versions of the studies I made out there to try to create something of the extraordinary presence and power of the buildings and the setting' (Cat. 111).

On the third day, James Hart Dyke accompanied the Prince on a 1,500 feet climb to the Tak Tsang monastery, or Tiger's Nest, where Tantric Buddhism was introduced to Bhutan. After a picnic lunch at a rest house, there was an opportunity for them both to

Cat. 110 *The Walk up to Misi Zam, Bhutan* 1998

paint the view. It was extremely hot and at an altitude of 10,000 feet, Hart Dyke began to feel giddy. Despite feeling sick for the rest of the day, he managed to paint two oils in the mountains, though tellingly, the predominant colour in both was black. The Prince also had difficulty with his watercolours: his paints dried too quickly in the sun and the dry air. The following day, after another morning walk with the Prince along the Drukgyel Valley, the artist flew back with the rest of the tour party via Kathmandu to RAF Brize Norton.

Cat. 111 *Paro Dzong, Bhutan* 1998

NOTES

Unless otherwise stated, all quotations from the tour artists are taken from interviews carried out by John Sheeran with the artists in their studios between March and May 1998.

1. HRH The Prince of Wales's Foreign Diaries, 2 May 1985, quoted in J. Dimbleby, *The Prince of Wales* (1994), p.430.
2. HRH The Prince of Wales, *HRH The Prince of Wales Watercolours* (1991), p.144.
3. Ibid., p.142.
4. Ibid., p.138.
5. All quotations from John Sergeant are taken from a letter from the artist to John Sheeran, 29 March 1998.
6. Letter from Toby Ward to HRH The Prince of Wales, 1 December 1993 (Cat. 88).
7. Toby Ward, *Sketchbook from the Gulf (ii)* 1993, p.25 (Cat. 83).
8. Letter from Toby Ward to HRH The Prince of Wales, 1 December 1993 (Cat. 88).

Catalogue of Works

All works in the exhibition are from the private collection of HRH The Prince of Wales, unless otherwise stated. Measurements are given in centimetres, height x width.

Watercolours by HRH The Prince of Wales

1. *View from Le Barroux, Provence* 1994
watercolour
14.3 x 22.5 cm
inscr. *C'94*
illust. p. 28

2. *Provençale Landscape* 1994
watercolour
17.3 x 24.8 cm
inscr. *C'94*
illust. p. 29

3. *Cypress Trees in Provence* 1995
watercolour
13.9 x 14.8 cm
inscr. *C'95*
illust. p. 30

4. *Provençale Landscape (ii)* 1996
watercolour
22 x 11.3 cm
inscr. *C'96*
illust. p. 30

5. *Provençale Evening in September* 1996
watercolour
14.5 x 21.3 cm
inscr. *C'96*
illust. p. 31

6. *Provençale Landscape* 1996
watercolour
21.5 x 27.6 cm
inscr. *C'96*
illust. p. 32

7. *Château Le Barroux, Provence (ii)* 1996
watercolour
21.4 x 13.7 cm
inscr. *C'96*
illust. p. 33

8. *Provençale Landscape (i)* 1996
watercolour
22 x 14.1 cm
inscr. *C'96*
illust. p. 33

9. *Looking towards Invercauld from Ballochbuie (i)* 1993
watercolour
9.6 x 11.5 cm
inscr. *C'93*
illust. p. 34

10. *From Auchtavan towards Invercauld* 1995
watercolour
11.5 x 17.3 cm
inscr. *C'95*
illust. p. 35

11. *Cairngorms from Glen Gelder, Balmoral* 1997
watercolour
18 x 28.8 cm
inscr. *C'97*
illust. p. 36

12. *Spring Evening on Deeside, Balmoral* 1997
watercolour
16.3 x 28.8 cm
inscr. *C'97*
illust. p. 37

13. *Ben Stack and Loch Stack, Sutherland* 1997
watercolour
22.2 x 27.8 cm
inscr. *C'97*
illust. p. 38

14. *View from Birkhall, Balmoral* 1997
watercolour
21.8 x 27.5 cm
inscr. *C'97*
illust. p. 39

15. *Scottish Scene, January (iv)* 1998
watercolour
22 x 28.4 cm
inscr. *C'98*
illust. p. 40

16. *Scottish Scene (i)* 1997
watercolour
22.2 x 28.5 cm
inscr. *C'97*
illust. p. 41

17. *Scottish Scene, January (v)* 1998
watercolour
20.2 x 28.1 cm
inscr. *C'98*
illust. p. 42

18. *Scottish Scene, January (vi)* 1998
watercolour
23 x 29.1 cm
inscr. *C'98*
illust. p. 43

19. *Scottish Scene, January (iii)* 1998
watercolour
22.7 x 29 cm
inscr. *C'98*
illust. p. 44

20. *View from the Hotel, Christchurch, New Zealand* 1994
watercolour
5.3 x 24.7 cm
inscr. *C'94*
illust. p. 45

21. *Corfu* 1995
watercolour
8.7 x 24.1 cm
inscr. *C'95*
illust. p. 45

22. *Monastery of St John the Divine, Patmos* 1993
pencil and watercolour
16.8 x 14.2 cm
inscr. *C'93*
illust. p. 46

23. *Monemvasia, Greece* 1994
watercolour
23 x 16.5 cm
inscr. *C'94*
illust. p. 46

24. *Samothraki* 1994
watercolour
24.1 x 16.4 cm
inscr. *C'94*
illust. p. 47

25. *Greek Landscape, Summer (x)* 1996
watercolour
17.1 x 11.6 cm
inscr. *C'96*
illust. p. 47

26. *Island of Senfos* 1995
watercolour
17.4 x 27.2 cm
inscr. *C'95*
illust. p. 48

27. *Greek Island Landscape, Fishing Boats* 1996
watercolour
14.8 x 22.2 cm
inscr. *C'96*
illust. p. 49

28. *Greek Landscape, Summer (vii)* 1996
watercolour
17.2 x 11.8 cm
inscr. *C'96*
illust. p. 50

29. *Greek Landscape, Summer (ix)* 1996
watercolour
19.6 x 14.1 cm
inscr. *C'96*
illust. p. 50

30. *Greek Landscape, Summer (iv)* 1996
watercolour
14.1 x 22.4 cm
inscr. *C'96*
illust. p. 51

31. *Greek Landscape, Summer (vi)* 1996
watercolour
16.6 x 27.5 cm
inscr. *C'96*
illust. p. 52

32. *Greek Landscape, Summer (i)* 1996
watercolour
14.6 x 27.6 cm
inscr. *C'96*
illust. p. 53

33. *Greek Landscape, Summer (ii)* 1996
watercolour
21.5 x 27.1 cm
inscr. *C'96*
illust. p. 54

34. *Roumeli Mountains near Gorge of Samaria* 1995
watercolour
16.8 x 27.2 cm
inscr. *C'95*
illust. p. 55

35. *Wadi Qaram from Sayq, Oman* 1995
watercolour
11.5 x 17.2 cm
inscr. *C'95*
illust. p. 56

36. *Moru Kopjes, Serengeti Plains, Tanzania* 1997
watercolour
22.5 x 29 cm
inscr. *C'97*
illust. p. 57

37. ***Ngorongoro from Hugo Hill, Serengeti Plains, Tanzania*** 1997
watercolour
22.5 x 28.8 cm
inscr. *C'97*
illust. p. 58

38. ***View towards Seronera Hills, Serengeti Plains, Tanzania*** 1997
watercolour
22.5 x 28.8 cm
inscr. *C'97*
illust. p. 59

39. ***Rufiji River from Mbuyuni Camp, Selous Game Reserve, Tanzania (i)*** 1997
watercolour
22.5 x 28.8 cm
inscr. *C'97*
illust. p. 60

40. ***Rufiji River, Selous Game Reserve, Tanzania*** 1997
watercolour
22.6 x 28.8 cm
inscr. *C'97*
illust. p. 61

41. ***Seronera Hills at Sunset, Serengeti Plains, Tanzania*** 1997
watercolour
15.7 x 28.7 cm
inscr. *C'97*
illust. p. 62

42. ***Rufiji River from Mbuyuni Camp, Selous Game Reserve, Tanzania (ii)*** 1997
watercolour
22.5 x 28.8 cm
inscr. *C'97*
illust. p. 63

43. ***The Hüreli, Klosters, Switzerland (ii)*** 1994
watercolour
14 x 24.1 cm
inscr. *C'94*
illust. p. 64

44. ***Above Klosters, Looking West, Other Side of Valley*** 1994
watercolour
14.1 x 24 cm
inscr. *C'94*
illust. p. 65

45. ***From the Hotel, Klosters*** 1995
watercolour
17 x 24.1 cm
inscr. *C'95*
illust. p. 66

46. ***View of Gotschna from Pany, Klosters*** 1996
watercolour
21.2 x 27.8 cm
inscr. *C'96*
illust. p. 67

47. ***Landscape, Sandringham*** 1995
watercolour
16.2 x 22.3 cm
inscr. *C'95*
illust. p. 68

48. ***Tetbury Church from Highgrove*** 1996
watercolour
14.8 x 20.2 cm
inscr. *C'96*
illust. p. 69

49. ***Norfolk Landscape in January*** 1997
watercolour
13.1 x 28.8 cm
inscr. *C'97*
illust. p. 70

50. ***View from Abbeystead, Lancashire*** 1997
watercolour
22.3 x 27.5 cm
inscr. *C'97*
illust. p. 71

Tour Artists

1985	John Ward	Italy
1986	Martin Yeoman	The Gulf
1989	Derek Hill	Turkey
	Martin Yeoman	Hong Kong
1990	Peter Kuhfeld	Nigeria, Cameroon and Tunisia
	Peter Kuhfeld	Japan
1991	Edmund Fairfax-Lucy	Brazil
	John Sergeant	Czechoslovakia
1992	Martin Yeoman	India and Nepal
1993	Peter Kuhfeld	Poland
	Toby Ward	The Gulf
1994	Tom Hallifax	USA and Hong Kong
1995	Emma Sergeant	Egypt and Morocco
	Derek Hill	Republic of Ireland
1995	Susannah Fiennes	Oman
1996	Derek Hill	Morocco
	Emma Sergeant	Central Asia
1997	India Jane Birley	Bangladesh
	Susannah Fiennes	Hong Kong
	Robert Wraith	Swaziland, Lesotho and South Africa
1998	James Hart Dyke	Sri Lanka, Nepal and Bhutan

Travels with the Prince *features the work of 10 of the tour artists.*

John Ward (born 1917)

51. ***The Quarterdeck, HMY Britannia*** 1985
pencil and watercolour on buff paper
23.2 x 31.3 cm
inscr. *John Ward.*
illust. p. 78

52. ***View from HMY Britannia*** 1985
pencil and watercolour on buff paper
22.9 x 31.5 cm
inscr. *John Ward / May 3rd*
illust. p. 76

53. ***View of Venice from HMY Britannia I*** 1985
pencil and watercolour
23 x 31.5 cm
inscr. *John Ward*
illust. p. 76

54. ***HMY Britannia*** 1985
pencil, pen and ink, and watercolour
31.2 x 23 cm
inscr. *John Ward*
illust. p. 75

55. ***View of Venice from HMY Britannia II*** 1985
pencil and watercolour on buff paper
31 x 47 cm
inscr. *John Ward / May 1985*
illust. p. 77

56. ***Illustrated Letter to HRH The Prince of Wales*** 12 October 1993
pencil, pen and ink and watercolour
31.4 x 23.6 cm
inscr. *John Ward*
illust. p. 79

Martin Yeoman (born 1953)

57. ***Coxswain Norrie, HMY Britannia*** 1986
pen and ink
21.2 x 16 cm
inscr. *22.11 / Yeoman*
illust. p. 83

58. ***Head Study of Gardener, British Council, Bahrain*** 1987
silverpoint and wash
21.5 x 16 cm
inscr. *Bahrain British Council / February 1987 / Yeoman*
illust. p. 84
exh. *Two Arabian Tours of the Middle East: Pictures by Martin Yeoman* (No. 51) Agnew's 1987

59. ***Blind Omani Fisherman, Ra's Al Hadd, Oman*** 1987
conté crayon and wash
26.1 x 17.2 cm
inscr. *Yeoman / 1 2 1987*
illust. p. 83
exh. *Two Arabian Tours of the Middle East: Pictures by Martin Yeoman* (No. 34) Agnew's 1987

60. ***A Dow on the Lagoon at Ra's Al Hadd, Oman*** 1987
oil on board
19.7 x 20 cm
illust. p. 81
exh. *Two Arabian Tours of the Middle East: Pictures by Martin Yeoman* (No. 19) Agnew's 1987

61. ***An Old Fort near Ra's Al Hadd, Oman*** 1987
oil on board
19.4 x 33.5 cm
illust. p. 80
exh. *Two Arabian Tours of the Middle East: Pictures by Martin Yeoman* (No. 20) Agnew's 1987

62. ***A Camel Grinding Sesame Seeds, Sana', Yemen*** 1987
oil on board
24.8 x 25.3 cm
illust. p. 82
exh. *Two Arabian Tours of the Middle East: Pictures by Martin Yeoman* (No. 32) Agnew's 1987

63. ***The Annapurna Range, Himalayas*** 1992
watercolour
15.5 x 25.3 cm
inscr. *Yeoman / Feb 1992*
illust. p. 84

DEREK HILL (born 1916)

64. ***Tory Island: West to the Lighthouse*** 1975
oil on board
13.2 x 31.1 cm
inscr. on back: *Tory / Sept 75 / DH / West to the Lighthouse*
illust. p. 85

65. ***St Nicolas Island, Fethiye, Turkey*** 1989
oil on board
13.4 x 20.7 cm
inscr. on back: *S.Nicolas Island / Fethiye / May 89 / DH*
illust. p. 86
Private Collection

66. ***Le Jardin de Monet,Giverny*** 1990
oil on board
13.8 x 20.7 cm
inscr. *DH* and on back: *Le Jardin de / Monet – Giverny / June 4 / 1990*
illust. p. 87
Private Collection

67. ***Kalahari*** 1991
oil on board
12 x 20.8 cm
inscr. on back: *an oil sketch / copied from a Kalahari / watercolour by / Prince Charles / DH August 91*
illust. p. 88
Private Collection

68. ***County Mayo*** 1995
oil on board
13.7 x 37.8 cm
inscr. on back: *Co. Mayo*
illust. p. 89
Private Collection

69. ***Château Le Barroux*** 1996
oil on board
16.5 x 19.2 cm
inscr. *DH*
illust. p. 90
Private Collection

70. ***Towards the Dentelles, Le Barroux*** 1996
oil on board
19.7 x 40.5 cm
illust. p. 90
Private Collection

PETER KUHFELD (born 1952)

71. ***The Durbar at Maiduguri, Nigeria*** 1990
oil on canvas
82.5 x 106.5 cm
inscr. *Kuhfeld*
illust. p. 93
exh. *Peter Kuhfeld: Recent Paintings* (No. 38) Agnew's 1991
Princes as Patrons (No. 214)
National Museum of Wales 1998

72. ***On the Road to Umuagbai Village, Rivers State, Nigeria*** 1990
oil on board
39.7 x 60.2 cm
inscr. *Kuhfeld* and on back of frame *On the Road to Umuagabi* (sic) *Village, Rivers State / March 1990*
illust. p. 92
exh. *Peter Kuhfeld: Recent Paintings* (No. 39) Agnew's 1991

73. ***Young Girl in a Blue Dress, Umuagbai Village, Nigeria*** 1990
oil on board
24 x 17.5 cm
inscr. *Kuhfeld* and on back of frame *Young girl in a blue dress, Umuagabi* (sic) *village / March 1990*
illust. p. 91
exh. *Princes as Patrons* (No. 213)
National Museum of Wales 1998

74. ***Tamanrasset, Algeria*** 1990
oil on board
38.5 x 55.5 cm
inscr. *Kuhfeld* and on back of frame *Tamanraset* (sic), *Algeria / March 1990*
illust. p. 94

75. ***The Capitol at Dougga, Tunisia*** 1990
oil on board
28.5 x 23 cm
inscr. *Kuhfeld*
illust. p. 95
exh. *Peter Kuhfeld: Recent Paintings* (No. 37) Agnew's 1991
Princes as Patrons (No. 212)
National Museum of Wales 1998

76. ***Morning in the Hatakeyama, Tokyo*** 1990
oil on board
31.5 x 44.5 cm
inscr. *Kuhfeld* and on back of frame *Hatakayama* (sic), *Tokyo / November 1990 / Peter Kuhfeld / Sir, wishing you a very happy birthday / Yours ever Peter*
illust. p. 96
exh. *Peter Kuhfeld: Recent Paintings* (No. 42) Agnew's 1991
Princes as Patrons (No. 217)
National Museum of Wales 1998

77. ***Town Hall, Gdansk, Poland*** 1993
oil on board
44.2 x 36.8 cm
inscr. *Kuhfeld* and on back of frame *Town Hall, Gdansk / May 1993 / Peter Kuhfeld*
illust. p. 97

JOHN SERGEANT (born 1937)

78. ***Illustrated Letter to HRH The Prince of Wales*** April 1990
pencil and ink, watercolour and gouache on buff paper
23.3 x 31.7 cm
illust. p. 98

79. ***Prague Skyline, Sv. Mikulas, Mala Strana*** 1991
ink and watercolour on buff paper
15.4 x 46.7 cm
inscr. *John Sergeant / Prague 1991*
illust. p. 99
exh. *Princes as Patrons* (No. 236)
National Museum of Wales 1998

80. ***Prague: Hradcany*** 1991
pen and ink and watercolour on buff paper
15.5 x 47.5 cm
inscr. *John Sergeant / Prague 1991*
illust. p. 99
exh. *Princes as Patrons* (No. 237)
National Museum of Wales 1998

81. ***Charles Bridge, Prague*** 1991
pen and ink and watercolour
16 x 23.3 cm
inscr. *John Sergeant / Prague 1991*
illust. p. 101

TOBY WARD (born 1965)

82. Sketchbook from the Gulf (i) 1993
Dimbleby Interview on top of the Dunes, The Empty Quarter
pencil and watercolour
10.5 x 15 cm (closed book)
inscr. *Dimbleby interview / on top of the dunes*
illust. p. 103
exh. *Princes as Patrons* (No. 241)
National Museum of Wales 1998

83. Sketchbook from the Gulf (ii) 1993
Lunch Given by The Amir of Kuwait and ***Visit to the Qurain Houses***
pencil, pen and watercolour
10.5 x 15 cm (closed book)
illust. p. 103
exh. *Princes as Patrons* (No. 241)
National Museum of Wales 1998

84. ***The Qurain Houses, Kuwait*** 1993
pencil and watercolour on coloured paper
15 x 21 cm
illust. p. 104

85. ***Film Crew, Qurain Houses, Kuwait*** 1993
pencil and watercolour
22.3 x 15 cm
illust. p. 102

86. ***The Empty Quarter*** 1993
pencil and watercolour
15 x 42 cm
illust. p. 105

87. ***Petra*** 1993
pencil and watercolour
15.1 x 40.5 cm
illust. p. 105

88. ***Illustrated Letter to HRH The Prince of Wales*** 1 December 1993
a) pencil, pen and ink and watercolour
22 x 17.1 cm
b) pencil, pen and ink and watercolour
22 x 17.1 cm
c) pencil, pen and ink and watercolour
22 x 17.1 cm
d) pencil, pen and ink and watercolour
22 x 17.1 cm
e) pencil, pen and ink and watercolour
22 x 17.1 cm
f) pencil, pen and ink and watercolour
22 x 17.1 cm
illust. p. 106

Emma Sergeant (born 1959)

89. ***Head Study, Egypt*** 1995
pencil
19.7 x 14.3 cm
inscr. *ES / 95*
illust. p. 107
exh. *Princes as Patrons* (No. 230)
National Museum of Wales 1998

90. ***Two Head Studies, Egypt*** 1995
a) pencil
19.7 x 14.3 cm
inscr. *ES / 95 / "Cheikh el Balad"*
b) pencil
19.7 x 14.3 cm
inscr. *ES / 95 / "Cheikh el Balad"*
illust. p. 108
exh. *Princes as Patrons* (No. 231)
National Museum of Wales 1998

91. ***HRH The Prince of Wales*** 1995
pencil
19.5 x 14.4 cm
inscr. *ES / 95*
illust. p. 109

92. ***Three Male Figure Studies, Central Asia*** 1996
a) black conté crayon
19.7 x 14.3 cm
inscr. *ES / 96*
b) black and purple conté crayon
19.7 x 14.3 cm
inscr. *ES / 96*
c) black conté crayon
19.7 x 14.3 cm
inscr. *ES / 96*
illust. p. 110

93. ***Three Female Studies, Central Asia*** 1996
a) black conté crayon
19.8 x 14.3 cm
inscr. *ES / 96*
b) black, brown and yellow conté crayon
19.8 x 14.3 cm
inscr. *ES / 96*
c) black conté crayon
19.8 x 14.3 cm
inscr. *Leena ES / 96*
illust. p. 111
exh. *Princes as Patrons* (No. 233)
National Museum of Wales 1998

Susannah Fiennes (born 1961)

94. ***Turbanned Head*** 1995
watercolour
28.8 x 21 cm
inscr. *S Fiennes '95 / Oman*
illust. p. 114
exh. *Princes as Patrons* (No. 195)
National Museum of Wales 1998

95. ***Four Standing Figures, Oman*** 1995
a) watercolour and brown conté crayon
29 x 13 cm
inscr. *S. Fiennes 95*
b) watercolour and brown conté crayon
29 x 13 cm
inscr. *S. Fiennes / 95*
c) watercolour and brown conté crayon
29 x 13 cm
inscr. *S. Fiennes 95*
d) watercolour and brown conté crayon
29 x 13 cm
inscr. *S. Fiennes 95*
illust. p. 115

96. ***HRH The Prince of Wales Painting in Oman*** 1995
watercolour
14.5 x 19.7 cm
inscr. *S. Fiennes '95*
illust. p. 113

97. ***HMY Britannia in Hong Kong Harbour*** 1997
watercolour
22.1 x 28.9 cm
inscr. *S Fiennes 29th June '97*
illust. p. 116
exh. *Princes as Patrons* (No. 198)
National Museum of Wales 1998

98. ***Christopher Patten Leaving Hong Kong*** 1997
watercolour
22.2 x 29.7 cm
inscr. *S. Fiennes*
illust. p. 117

Robert Wraith (born 1952)

99. ***Studies of Dancing Figure, Ngculwini, Swaziland*** 1997
pen and ink, watercolour and sepia wash
18.9 x 13.8 cm
inscr. *Ngculwini / Swaziland / Robbie Wraith / 1997*
illust. p. 119

100. ***Coronation of King Letsie III, Lesotho: Figure on Horse*** 1997
pen and ink, watercolour and sepia wash
13.1 x 18.5 cm
inscr. *Coronation of King Letsie III / Lesotho 31st October 1997 Robbie Wraith*
illust. p. 118
exh. *Princes as Patrons* (No. 243)
National Museum of Wales 1998

101. ***Mahlamba Ndlopfu, Lunch with President Mandela*** 1997
red conté crayon
18.4 x 13.7 cm
inscr. *Mahlamba Ndlopfu, Pretoria / Robbie Wraith. 1 Nov. 1997.*
illust. p. 121
exh. *Princes as Patrons* (No. 244)
National Museum of Wales 1998

102. ***The Spice Girls in Concert in Aid of the Nations Trust, Johannesburg*** 1997
pen and ink and watercolour
12.5 x 18.8 cm
inscr. *Robbie Wraith 1997*
illust. p. 120
exh. *Princes as Patrons* (No. 245)
National Museum of Wales 1998

103. ***Helicopter to Dukuduku*** 1997
pen and ink and watercolour
18.6 x 13.5 cm
inscr. *In the helicopter to DukuDuku* (sic) */ Robbie Wraith 1997.*
illust. p. 120
exh. *Princes as Patrons* (No. 247)
National Museum of Wales 1998

104. ***Studies of Woman with British Flag, Crossroads, Capetown*** 1997
pen and ink with watercolour and sepia wash
18.5 x 13.3 cm
inscr. *Cape Town, 1997 / Robbie Wraith*
illust. p. 122
exh. *Princes as Patrons* (No. 248)
National Museum of Wales 1998

105. ***Standing Figure, Crossroads, Capetown*** 1997
pen and ink with watercolour and sepia wash
20.5 x 14.2 cm
inscr. *Crossroads / Capetown 1997 Robert Wraith*
illust. p. 122
exh. *Princes as Patrons* (No. 249)
National Museum of Wales 1998

106. ***Johannesburg*** 1997
pen and ink and watercolour
20.4 x 14.2 cm
inscr. *Johannesburg / 1997 / Robert Wraith*
illust. p. 122
exh. *Princes as Patrons* (No. 250)
National Museum of Wales 1998

James Hart Dyke (born 1966)

107. ***View towards Himalayas, Nepal*** 1998
oil on panel
15 x 30 cm
inscr. *James Hart Dyke 1998* and on back *View towards Himalayas, Nepal Sunday 8th Feb 1998*
illust. p. 124

108. ***View South of Kathmandu, Nepal*** 1998
oil on panel
15 x 30 cm
inscr. *James Hart Dyke 1998* and on back *View South of Katmandu, Nepal 1998 / Sunday 8th Feb 1998*
illust. p. 125

109. ***Paro Dzong, Bhutan*** 1998
oil on panel
15 x 30 cm
inscr. *James Hart Dyke 1998* and on back *Paro Dzong, Bhutan / Tuesday 10th Feb 1998*
illust. p. 126

110. ***The Walk up to Misi Zam, Bhutan*** 1998
oil on panel
15 x 30 cm
inscr. *James Hart Dyke 1998* and on back *The Walk up to Misi Zam / Bhutan / Thursday 12th Feb 1998*
illust. p. 127

111. ***Paro Dzong, Bhutan*** 1998
oil on canvas
66 x 106.2 cm
inscr. *James Hart Dyke / Bhutan 1998* and on back *Paro Dzong, Bhutan*
illust. p. 128

Works in exhibition by non-tour artists

John Napper (born 1916)

112. ***Study for Portrait of HRH The Prince of Wales*** 1994
pencil and wash
70.2 x 65 cm
inscr. *John Napper / 1994*
illust. p. 144

Angela Conner

113. ***HRH The Prince of Wales*** 1995
bronze
48.5 x 32 x 22 cm
inscr. $^{2}/_{10}$ Conner
exh. *Princes as Patrons* (No. 253)
National Museum of Wales 1998
not illustrated

Illustrations

Catalogue Contributors

Susan Morris is a writer, art historian and specialist in British watercolours. She has written extensively on Turner, Girtin, and 18th and 19th century European art, and is a former editor of *Sotheby's Preview* and *The Antique Collector*.

John Sheeran, curator of ***Travels with the Prince***, worked in fine art museums throughout the 1980s, including seven years as Keeper of Dulwich Picture Gallery. He set up the specialist art consultancy Sheeran Lock with Imogen Lock in 1990.

Fig. 16 *HRH The Prince of Wales painting in Bhutan 1998*

Select Bibliography

Burford, Brian Sinfield Gallery, *Robert Wraith* (exhibition catalogue 1994)

Cardiff, The National Museum of Wales, *Princes as Patrons* (exhibition catalogue 1998)

D. Coombs, 'Queen Elizabeth's Collection', *The Antique Collector* (Aug 1990), 30-7

J. Dimbleby, *The Prince of Wales* (1994)

G. Gowrie, *Derek Hill: An Appreciation* (1987)

E. Grice, 'The Prince and the painter' (Susannah Fiennes), *Daily Telegraph* (18 June 1997)

J. Halsby, *The Art of Diana Armfield* (1995)

J. Halsby and Peter Kuhfeld, 'The Artist in Conversation', *The Artist* (Nov 1991) 21-23

London, Thos. Agnew & Sons, *Emma Sergeant: Drinks at Milapote: Family and Friends* (exhibition catalogue 1984)

London, Thos. Agnew & Sons, *Two Tours in the Middle East: Pictures by Martin Yeoman* (exhibition catalogue 1987)

London, Thos. Agnew & Sons, *Salute to Turner* (exhibition catalogue 1989)

London, Thos. Agnew & Sons, *John Ward R.A. Retrospective Exhibition* (exhibition catalogue 1990)

London, Thos. Agnew & Sons, *Peter Kuhfeld: Recent Paintings* (exhibition catalogue 1991)

London, Thos. Agnew & Sons, *Emma Sergeant: Orpheus and the Underworld* (exhibition catalogue 1994)

London, Albemarle Gallery, *John Napper: Recent Paintings* (exhibition catalogue 1991)

London, Christie's, *The National Trust's Centenary Exhibition* (exhibition catalogue 1995)

London, Colnaghi, *Derek Hill: Favourites in Retrospect* (exhibition catalogue 1994)

London, Fine Art Society, *Emma Sergeant: Dolphins* (exhibition catalogue 1998)

London, Hazlitt Gooden & Fox, *Three Contemporary Artists: John Sergeant, Jehan Daly & John Ward* (exhibition catalogue 1994)

London, Hazlitt Gooden & Fox, *John Sergeant: Drawings* (exhibition catalogue 1996)

London, Hazlitt Gooden & Fox, *John Ward in Rome: Recent Drawings* (exhibition catalogue 1996)

London, Hazlitt Gooden & Fox, *John Ward on Tour: Recent Drawings* (exhibition catalogue 1998)

London, John Martin Gallery, *Robbie Wraith* (exhibition catalogue 1995)

London, National Gallery, *The Queen's Pictures*, ed. C. Lloyd (exhibition catalogue 1991)

London, W.H. Patterson Gallery, *Peter Kuhfeld: Recent Paintings* (exhibition catalogue 1996)

London, Sotheby's, *HRH The Prince of Wales: An Exhibition of Watercolours to Mark the 25th Anniversary of His Investiture* (exhibition catalogue 1994)

London, Sotheby's, *The Artist and the Country House from the Fifteenth Century to the Present Day* (exhibition catalogue 1996)

London, Tate Gallery, *John Piper*, ed. D. Fraser Jenkins (exhibition catalogue 1983-4)

T. Mackintosh-Smith, *Yemen: Travels in Dictionary Land* (1997)

New Haven, Yale Center for British Art, *Crown Pictorial*, ed. L. Colley (exhibition catalogue 1990)

New York, Newhouse Galleries; Thos. Agnew & Sons, London, *Emma Sergeant: Gods* (exhibition catalogue 1996)

J. Norrie, 'Chinese Characters' (Susannah Fiennes), *Hong Kong Tatler* (Aug 1994), 86-88

Norwich, Norwich School of Art Gallery, *Peter Greenham* (exhibition catalogue 1984-5)

Philadelphia, Philadelphia Museum of Art; Tate Gallery, London, *Sir Edwin Landseer* (exhibition catalogue 1981-2)

HRH The Prince of Wales, *A Vision of Britain* (1989)

HRH The Prince of Wales, *HRH The Prince of Wales Watercolours* (1991)

HRH The Prince of Wales, 'Painting with plants', *Perspectives* (June 1995), 30-5

HRH The Prince of Wales and C. Clover, *Highgrove: Portrait of an Estate* (1993)

HM Queen Victoria, *Our Life in the Highlands* (William Kimber, London, edition 1968)

J. Reid, *Edward Seago: The Landscape Art* (1991)

J. Roberts, *Royal Artists from Mary Queen of Scots to the Present Day* (1987)

Salisbury, The National Trust's Foundation For Art at Mompesson House, *Martin Yeoman: Selected Works* (exhibition catalogue 1994)

Sana', The National Gallery of Yemen, *Yeoman's Yemen* (exhibition catalogue 1997)

J. Ward, *The Paintings of John Ward* (1991)

M. Warner, *Queen Victoria's Sketchbook* (1979)

Welbeck, The Harley Gallery; Tenbury Wells, Burford House Gallery; London, Colnaghi, *John Napper* (exhibition catalogue 1996)

Cat. 71 Peter Kuhfeld *The Durbar at Maiduguri, Nigeria* 1990 (detail)

JOHN NAPPER
1997

The Prince of Wales's Charitable Foundation

The Prince of Wales's Charitable Foundation, formerly known as The Prince of Wales's Charities Trust, was established in 1979 and distributes money each year to benefit a wide range of causes throughout the world. The causes and projects supported by the Foundation reflect The Prince of Wales's personal interests. Particular assistance has been given over the years to projects in the fields of healthcare, disadvantaged young people, educational initiatives, the environment and the arts.

A significant part of the Foundation's income is derived from royalties from the sale of books by The Prince of Wales and of lithographs made from his own watercolours, together with donations made from Duchy Originals Ltd, which he established in 1990. The Foundation receives an ever-increasing number of requests for assistance. Recent beneficiaries have included the Bristol Cancer Health Centre, The Macmillan Nurse Appeal, The Royal Shakespeare Company, The Norfolk Churches Trust, The Henry Doubleday Research Association, The War Widows Association, and The Royal College of Music.

Last year, The Prince of Wales's Charitable Foundation made donations totalling £300,000. Income raised through the sale of this catalogue and related merchandise will be donated to The Prince of Wales's Charitable Foundation.

Fig. 17 John Napper *Highgrove House* 1997
Given by the artist for sale in aid of
The Prince of Wales's Charitable Foundation

Hampton Court Palace

Travels with the Prince is being held in the magnificent Cartoon Gallery at Hampton Court Palace. Home to some of Britain's most famous kings and queens, the Palace has been the setting for many great events during nearly 500 years of royal history. Viewed from the west, Hampton Court is still the red brick Tudor palace of Henry VIII (1509-1547); from the east it presents the stately Baroque façade designed by Sir Christopher Wren for William III (1689-1702). The sumptuous interiors reflect the changing tastes of its royal residents and are furnished with great works of art, many displayed in their original settings. The Palace is surrounded by beautiful gardens and extensive parkland, set by the river Thames.

A richly decorated gallery, exclusively for the use of Henry VIII, already existed in Tudor times, but it was William III's enthusiasm for art that turned Hampton Court into the palace of the arts that it has become today. He created two new galleries and allowed artists to copy works of art. Important 16th and 17th century Old Master paintings can be viewed today in the Wolsey Rooms and the Renaissance Picture Gallery.

The Cartoon Gallery is one of the first purpose-built picture galleries in Britain. Built by Wren to display Raphael's *Acts of the Apostles*, it now houses 17th century copies of Raphael's large drawings, the originals having been given by Prince Albert to the Victoria and Albert Museum in 1865. It is the first time that the Cartoon Gallery has been used for such an exhibition. This lofty interior has been specially transformed for ***Travels with the Prince*** into a series of more intimate exhibition galleries, while still respecting Wren's architecture.

Today many of the State Apartments are being restored and furnished to reflect the lives of their principal royal residents. Outside the building a music festival, flower show and many improvements to the historic gardens all add to the busy life of the palace for its many visitors.

Fig. 18 Hampton Court Palace

166
165

Asprey & Garrard

The historic English companies Asprey and Garrard were brought together into one business on September 1st, 1998. Their home is the splendid Bond Street showroom, that was first occupied by Asprey in 1847, as well as showrooms in New York, Beverly Hills and Paris. Both companies have a heritage steeped in the design and manufacture of extraordinary objects, whose style has brought them international recognition for over two hundred years.

Innovation in design has always been the style of Asprey and Garrard and many historical landmarks for both companies now unite them as the strongest English luxury goods company for the 21st Century.

Asprey's revolutionary lightweight dressing case attracted Queen Victoria's attention at the Great Exhibition of 1851, and in 1862 Asprey won the first of its many Royal warrants. At the same Great Exhibition, Garrard displayed extensive collections of commissions, including the ornate Cowes Yacht Race Cup, which was presented for the first time by Queen Victoria that same year.

The magic of Asprey & Garrard today is the extraordinary level of personal service. For bespoke jewellery, imaginative silver-work, custom-made leather accessories, and unique and imaginative objets d'art, clients draw upon the expertise of the Asprey & Garrard craftsmen and designers situated in workshops above the showroom in Bond Street. A grooming case in alligator hide? A custom-designed hand-painted dinner service? A sterling silver computer mouse? The reply invariably echoes the Asprey & Garrard motto – "It can be done."

Fig. 19 James Hart Dyke
Asprey & Garrard, New Bond Street 1998
Given by the artist for sale in aid of
The Prince of Wales's Charitable Foundation

Cat. 112 John Napper
Study for Portrait of HRH The Prince of Wales 1994
(Collection of HRH The Prince of Wales)